How to Really Learn a Language

Jeff Martin

Author's Note

If after reading through this book, you feel like it has helped you in any way, please remember to leave a positive review online. This will help increase exposure and ultimately result in more people discovering their ability to learn languages. Also, don't forget to join my mailing list at www.howtoreallylearnalanguage.com

-Jeff

Contents

Acknowledgements

I owe so much to so many people, including my wife, daughters, parents, grandparents, many other relatives, friends, colleagues, coworkers, teachers and language students. Without these people, their support, input, and overall participation in my life's work, this book wouldn't have been possible.

6

Introduction

Imagine that you arrive late to a magic show. All the seats are taken, but you've already paid your entry fee. The theater staff offers you a chance to watch from a seat backstage and refunds your money. You gladly accept, take your seat, and start watching the magician perform a card trick. At one point during the trick, you observe a subtle hand movement made by the magician that everyone else in the audience would be unable to see.

You realize he has cards up his sleeve, yet everyone else perceives his trick as magic. Several different sleight of hand tricks occur in this manner, and you happen to see the hidden movements of each trick, revealing the secrets behind them all. You are the only person in the room with this visual advantage

After the show, the magician gives a question and answer forum for the audience. Most questions have to do with the way certain tricks were performed. Instead of answering, the magician asks the audience if anyone can figure out the answers. You just happen to know how he performed every trick, so you speak up to reveal the magician's secrets. After the show, several people approach you astonished at your "ability" and "gift" of discernment and deduction. They have no idea that you aren't gifted at all. You simply saw the show from a different perspective.

People often accuse me of having a gift for languages.
I'm just trying to invite them backstage. I guess I should
introduce myself, then. My name is Jeff Martin. I am a
Master Certified Spanish Court Interpreter. I currently
have no college degree. I have never lived in a Spanish-
speaking country nor household. I, like many of you,
took Spanish for a few semesters in high school, but was
still unable to speak and understand the spoken language.
Despite all of this, I was somehow able to pass one of the
most difficult language tests in existence to become a
Master Certified Court Interpreter.

I first began to really learn foreign languages at the
age of 17. A few months after graduating high school, I
went on a youth mission trip to Brazil. After just three
days of being in Brazil, I found myself being able to hold

basic conversations in Portuguese. After our two-week trip, we returned to the U.S., and I immediately looked for Brazilians to practice with. I became friends with several native Brazilians in my local community, stayed in constant contact with my friends in Brazil, and quickly progressed in Portuguese.

Later that year, I started my first full time job working at a turkey plant. The first thing I noticed was the massive amount of migrant Hispanic workers. At first, I had no desire to learn Spanish, but after my one-week orientation, I was introduced to one of my supervisors. During a conversation with him, we were interrupted by one of the Hispanic workers, and I witnessed my boss speak what seemed to be fluent Spanish with ease! Amazed, I asked him where he had learned it. He replied that he just picked it up at the plant by speaking with the workers and had become fluent in seven months!

It was at that point that I made a goal to test my abilities and become fluent in less time than he had. After three months, I had become fluent enough that many supervisors would ask me to interpret for their staff meetings. While working there, I was exposed to other languages as well. From other migrant workers I learned the basics in Chinese, Korean, and a Mayan dialect called Mam. Thirteen months after I started my first full time job as a factory worker, I left in order to pursue a career more related to my newfound passion for languages.

People ask me all the time how to learn a language. In the past, I would simply tell them the names of some language courses that I like. Very few of the people who have asked me for advice in the past ever reached fluency, which is what led me to write this book.

When I first began learning foreign languages, people told me I had a gift. I believed that to be true for a long time until I met a guy who ended up becoming one of my best friends. I first met Derek Miller while I was working as a guitar salesman at Musician's Toy Store, in Jacksonville, NC. By that point, I had already become fluent in English, Portuguese, Spanish, Italian, and had learned the basics in French, German, Swiss German, Mandarin, Hebrew, and had dabbled in several other languages. So, it was easy for me to believe that I had a gift, especially since I hadn't met anyone else who could do what I do.

Since Derek was immediately impressed with my language abilities he, like most people I met, asked me how I did it. I honestly never really knew how to answer that question, so I simply recommended a particular language course that I had recently stumbled across. The course that I recommended to Derek was an all audio course that I had used before my first trip to Europe in 2003. I recommended it to everyone that ever asked me about languages. Not a single person who I had recommended the course to became fluent, which always baffled me. It was easiest to assume that everyone was right about me having a gift for languages.

The following year, after I had begun working as an interpreter, Derek called me out of the blue and asked me for the name of that course I had recommend to him. He said he wanted to learn Spanish. I gladly gave him the information and a few tips on how to use the course. A few weeks later, Derek and I were having phone conversations in Spanish! While he was going through the course, and obviously afterwards, he spent lots of time with native speakers and became really fluent. A few months after our first Spanish conversation, he landed a position as a medical interpreter for a local clinic! That was when something in me shifted. If Derek could do it, and I could do it, couldn't anyone?

Thus began the long process of pondering and analysis. I decided to start giving Spanish lessons to my coworkers to see if I could discover how people learn foreign languages. The problem was that not one person had success in my class. It wasn't until years later that I realized I had set them up for failure by teaching them the Spanish alphabet on day one. In retrospect I believe that each one of them would be super fluent in Spanish or any other language by now if they had only been given the information you're reading in this book. It wasn't until my wife and I had children that I finally began to understand how people learn languages. The process became quite obvious to me while going through the experience of teaching our first daughter how to speak. I feel bad for my first language students. Right now, they are probably a lot like you: led to believe that some people have it and most don't.

Over the years I have heard a plethora of excuses as to why a person cannot learn a foreign language. I'm sure you've heard those myths too. I personally believe that those myths began when the current system for learning languages was established. When a person sets out to complete a task and fails, what is their natural response? Justification. Most people can't cope with failure, so they justify to themselves why such failure occurred, usually blaming external forces beyond their control: I'm too old. I started too late in life. I am not gifted. I've never lived in a foreign country. I wasn't exposed to the language before a certain age.

Let's take a moment to consider a scenario. If you were the same race you are now, but were born and raised in China, wouldn't you speak Chinese? What if you moved to Syria at the age of 5? Wouldn't you also speak Arabic? Certainly! But what about now? Don't you have the same body and mind that you just claimed was capable of learning Chinese and Arabic? Picture yourself standing face to face with a Chinese person. Don't they have a similar anatomy to yours (aside from gender, perhaps)? Aren't their speech organs similar to yours? Then why do you believe that you can't learn to produce the same language sounds as them?

Over the years I have met a handful of people that can speak other languages and sound just like a native. They all have one thing in common. They spent a considerable amount of time with native speakers. Are those people more talented at language than you? I don't think so. I personally believe that you are, in part, multilingual.

How many versions of English can you speak? For example, you could be talking on the phone to your best friend, using mostly "street slang," then on the same day go to court to pay a ticket, where most of the language you would use is of a high register and filled with legal terms and formalities. That evening you might attend a political rally, followed by a church service. Later that night you read your 5-year-old daughter a bedtime story. You would speak in at least five different registers of

English on just that day alone.

It might not seem like that big of a difference to you, but try speaking street slang in the courtroom or talking politics with your 5-year-old. Each situation calls for a different "version" of English. Does this make you multilingual? Perhaps not, but the complexity of your language abilities in your native language is obvious. You see, in essence, **you are a language master**. Your ability to learn your first language amazes me much more than myself or anyone else learning a foreign language. I believe that if we apply the same skill set and techniques that we used naturally to learn our own language to learning a foreign language, we can become just as fluent.

So now I ask you to come with me on a journey- a

language journey, if you will. You just may catch

yourself believing in you.

01 System Failure

ASK YOURSELF THESE TWO QUESTIONS: How many bilingual people do I know? How did they become bilingual?

Let's pretend you are planning a trip to Mexico next summer, so you decide to learn Spanish. How would you learn it? Most people would either register for a Spanish class or buy a course, right? Chances are you or someone you know have already done so. In fact, millions of people have taken foreign language classes or purchased courses, but how many of them have achieved fluency?

Shortly after I became fluent in Spanish, I had an experience that began to open up my eyes to the existence of a problem in the way languages are being taught. One night, while I was at work, one of the plant section managers called me over to him, asking me to speak Spanish to another employee. By then, I was quite used to people prompting me to speak Spanish in order to show off my ability, so I thought nothing of it. I was shocked, however, when he responded back to me in Spanish. He spoke very slowly, and with a heavy American accent. When I asked him how he had learned it, he said that he was a Spanish major in college. I was astounded! He had a degree in Spanish but sounded like a beginner!

Since then I have encountered countless similar situations. A friend of mine who is an attorney, Tyrell Clemons, once told me that I inspired him, because every time he sees me interpreting he wishes he could speak Spanish. He added that he studied Spanish for eight years in school and still can't speak it. When Hispanic clients come to his office, the only thing he can say to them is "*un momento.*"

Working as a court interpreter, I've met many more attorneys that studied Spanish in college, but only a few of them are even close to being fluent. But, why? Attorneys are highly educated, and most are extremely intelligent. There must be an explanation.

I could list hundreds of other examples of people who have "learned" a language either by taking classes or purchasing a course, most with little to no actual results, which points out the existence of a serious problem -

where are all the bilinguals?

Of all the people I know, only a very small percentage of them are bilingual, most of whom are either children of immigrants to the U.S., have lived in a foreign country, worked closely with or have been in a relationship with one or more native speakers. I have yet to find one person that has become fluent by using a course or taking a class. Can this be explained by simply claiming that languages are hard to learn? Do you have to be gifted to learn languages?

Almost everyone I know speaks a language. You are not born speaking your native tongue, rather you must learn how to do so. This skill is not one that is lost after childhood. In fact, it is refined over and over again until you graduate high school or college. Even after that, you have to learn the jargon required to function in any given situation in life. Also, new words are constantly being introduced into our vocabularies via technology, pop culture, cinema, television, literature, the internet, etc.

You see, we are natural language learners, and our mastery of language grows ever increasingly until we eventually lose our mental faculties due to old age or illness. The problem is not that we are unable to learn languages; rather, we need to become aware of how we learned our first language and apply that knowledge to learning other languages. The best way to achieve said awareness is to observe how children learn language. Better yet, let's look back at how we learned our first language.

Before we were born, at around 18 weeks after

conception, our ears were developed enough to hear. It was at this point that language first began to make an impression on us. Through our sense of hearing, we are aware of an endless stream of sounds, a large percentage of them being spoken words. Obviously at this point we don't even know what language is, but nevertheless we are perceiving it. We spend the next 4.5 months or so mostly listening.

Once we are born we are no longer surrounded by embryonic fluid, therefore sounds become clearer than ever. Plus, we now have the ability to make sounds. On day one we begin to use our mouths to cry, laugh, babble, etc. We are also aware of sounds that emanate from the mouths of others. We recognize Mom's voice right away, as hers was the loudest while in the womb.

As babies, we are constantly being coached in

speaking. Our parents hold us close and speak directly to us. They speak slowly and often use "baby talk," repeating the simplest of words; such as "mama" or "dada." We have the wonderful advantage of face time, and we marvel as we watch their mouths move to produce the words, as well as the facial expressions that go along with them.

Over the first several months of life we gradually develop the ability of mimicry. That's when the magic begins to happen. We've already been able to identify some things through context, but now that we can mimic, we are able to learn at an exponential rate. The words we mimic produce responses in other people. When we say "mama" our mother responds with such delight. These responses trigger emotions in us and help us to identify people, places, and things in our life.

We then continue to progress by listening, repeating, and connecting sounds (words) with objects, people, and actions. We eventually begin to group words together. First, two words at a time, then three, then four, until we are finally able to speak in sentences. With time, practice, listening, and helpful coaching, our accent and pronunciation improve, causing us to sound less like a toddler, and more like a native speaker. This process continues until we are finally fluent enough to begin kindergarten. It is at this magical time that we are taught how to draw sounds.

By the age of 5, most of us already know about 5,000 words. Around this age we begin school, start to learn how to read, write, and use proper grammar. When we learned the alphabet, we were taught to assign sounds of our native tongue to each letter or combination of letters, sounds that we had already learned how to produce. Those are the same sounds we can mentally "hear" while reading silently.

Compare this to the common classroom approach to learning foreign languages. The student learns the new alphabet on or about day one. If the alphabet uses Roman script, the student tries desperately to assign new sounds to letters that they have been pronouncing a certain way their whole life, which is extremely difficult. Most students have a natural tendency to pronounce the new alphabet with sounds of their native language, the only language sounds they have mastered. Once the alphabet is "learned," the student proceeds to learn to read and write in the new language but continues to pronounce the words using his or her native language sounds. (When they see the Spanish word *estar*, mentally they are still hearing English sounds.) Added to this almost unavoidable trap of mispronunciation is the company of peer learners, the accents of whom are no better. This fosters a sense of social proof, subconsciously leading the student to accept this way of speaking the foreign language. Furthermore, if the student receives passing grades in said class, they can only gather that they are doing a good job. To make things worse, there is a likelihood the teacher is not a native speaker, having studied along this same path and received a college degree, yet never having mastered the correct pronunciation, perpetuating this verbal folly. If a student happens to be in a classroom in which the instructor is a native speaker, and focuses on correct pronunciation, they may be considered luckier than most. However, being introduced to the written language in the beginning will serve to be an immense obstacle.

This approach results in little to no comprehension of the language when spoken by natives, little to no verbal fluency, and almost always a horrible accent. Although the student may become proficient in reading and writing, the lack of focus on listening and speaking leads to the common proclamation, "I can read it better than I can speak it."

Most self-study language courses follow a similar approach, in that the learner is exposed to the written language from day one. However, in this case there is no live instructor. Probably the only advantage the classroom setting has over self-study is the human interaction and correction from the instructor, provided the instructor sounds like a native speaker.

Compare the average beginner language student to a 5-

year-old native speaker. Who is more prepared to start kindergarten? After all, this common classroom approach to foreign language instruction is almost like a second kindergarten, only in a foreign language. What is the difference in experiences between a toddler and an adult learner? The toddler is learning from a different source; native speakers. If we consider that the toddler sleeps an average of 10 hours per day, 5 years equates to 25,500 waking hours spent mostly around other people, who spend much of their time communicating with other native speakers. Therefore, the 5-year-old's main advantage is the massive exposure to the language as it is spoken naturally by natives. They have received language coaching consistently throughout their life to this point and are therefore quite proficient. Additionally, their curiosity about life in general causes an endless supply of questions to ask, and be answered in kind,

perpetuating their learning of life concepts and the

language with which to describe them.

The beginner foreign language student, however, does

not have any of the aforementioned advantages.

Therefore, it is unfair to expect them to be able to

perform at any level of proficiency no matter how many

classes they take.

If the currently accepted approach to language

learning is inadvertently yet inevitably designed for you

to fail, how then, can you expect to really learn a new

language? I believe the answer is simple. You've done it

once before. Let's do it again.

02 Bridging the Gap

If the current system of foreign language instruction is failing, producing almost zero bilingual individuals, what options do you have as a foreign language learner? In my opinion, the first thing to understand is that traditional as well as most modern methods are not incorrect in their approach to language instruction; rather, they are simply misplaced. As I hopefully have established by now, foreign language classes and most courses are set up sort of like an advanced adult kindergarten, yet in a foreign language. It is simply absurd to start at that point, skipping the foundational skills that we learned before we entered school.

The pivotal point in our journey to master our native language is when we learn how to read and write. Our literacy skills usually begin to develop in kindergarten and continue to develop for the next 12-16+ years of school. But why do we begin in kindergarten? Before entering grade school, a child must possess certain social, motor, language, as well as other skills. Linguistically speaking, most 5-year-olds are basically fluent in their native language, possessing a limited vocabulary of around 5,000 words, and a basic understanding of grammar. They may not speak perfectly, but they can get their point across. It took about five years of work to get to the point of qualifying to learn how to read and write.

As a beginner, your focus should be to acquire similar language skills as those of a 5-year-old before you learn to read or write in the foreign language. What does this mean? Do you have to spend five years learning a language from natives before learning to read? Would an adult learn faster or slower than a native toddler?

Five thousand words may seem like a lot to learn, but it took the average kindergartener around five years to do so. As an adult, learning five thousand words over a span of five years would seem quite slow, learning at a rate of about two to three words per day. The reason it took so long for the average five-year-old to learn this amount of vocabulary was because they spent those five years simultaneously learning all about the world around them, developing mentally, physically, and just beginning to develop emotionally, all while learning to speak his or her native language to be able to communicate.

On the other hand, the adult learner is simply assigning new sounds to existing concepts, since he or she is already fully developed and experienced in the matters of daily life. Therefore, the process of learning a new word can be much quicker rather than learning a whole new concept, including the vocabulary to describe it. For example, as a toddler learns the word couch, what takes place? First, they must have an experience or set of experiences that involve multiple senses, connecting as much sensory information as possible to the sound and meaning of the word to fully identify this object. A toddler has a lot of different yet intimate experiences with a couch. Chances are the parents and or siblings spend a great amount of time sitting on the couch, provoking the toddler to approach the couch to communicate with whoever is on it, not to mention the time spent sitting on the couch with family. After some time, this toddler knows what the couch looks like, feels like, smells like, and even sounds like when being utilized. Perhaps they have been to other homes and have seen all different types of couches, or even visited a furniture store where there is an endless ocean of couches, monumental in daily life, since a considerable amount of family time is spent in the living room. To the toddler, this concept is called couch. It has deep meaning in their life.

Yet as an adult, if you learn the word "couch" in a foreign language, the process is much simpler. You hear and perceive the word, connect it with your personal concept of a couch in your mind, and you learn to produce the sounds that make up the word. Or perhaps you learn how to speak the word before you learn it's meaning. Either way, you pull up the memory, perhaps subconsciously, of the concept of a couch in your mind. Most of the work was done years ago. This is simply a new way to describe your experience. So, the adult has an obvious speed advantage. Yet, most adults hinder their learning curve by starting at the wrong point, reading before speaking.

The question probably lingering in your mind at this point is how can you become "kindergarten ready" in a foreign language without learning how to read or write? To me, the answer is simple; observe how we learned our first language and repeat the process as closely as possible. To recap the process discussed in chapter one, here is a list of the steps you probably took to master your native language:

1. You became aware of sounds emanating from your mouth and the mouths of others and spent lots of time watching and listening.
2. You gradually developed the ability of mimicry.
3. Mimicry produced responses in others, which helped you begin to identify the people and objects in your daily life.
4. You progressed by listening, repeating, and connecting sounds with objects, actions, and your basic needs.
5. You began to combine words into groups to further express yourself.
6. With time and practice, listening, and helpful coaching, you began to sound like a native speaker.

7. This process continued until you were fluent enough to begin kindergarten.

8. You were taught to "draw sounds" (reading and writing) as well as grammar basics.

9. Through years of study you eventually achieved mastery of your native tongue.

Obviously, you can't be reborn into another culture, but you can still approach learning a new language in a similar way if you understand the process. First you listened, then you learned to mimic. You connected words with meaning. You gradually built your vocabulary while being coached by natives. After some time, you qualified to learn to read and write.

As a foreign language learner, do you need to have learned 5,000 words before learning to read and write?

Probably not. It would be better to set a short-term goal of around 500 words. If at that point you have mastered your pronunciation, then go for it. Learn to read and write. On the other hand, if you still struggle with your pronunciation, wait until you have learned closer to 1,000 words. The key is to be honest with yourself about how you sound. As will be repeated several times in this book, **it's important to record yourself speaking the foreign language**.

But how do you go about learning your first 500-1000 words without using the written language? Good question. A better question is, why weren't you given a manual at birth explaining how to learn your native language? Simply put, you didn't need one. You had the source of the language readily available - native speakers.

Language is something we initially

learned from other people. Why

should that change when it comes to

learning a foreign language?

03 Clean Slate

Step One – Listening

—Where did you learn our language?

— I listened!

The 13th Warrior

I remember a scene from the movie listed above as one
of the first impactful moments in my life, as far as

language is concerned. Ahmed Ibn Fahdlan had been immersed in a group of Vikings who spoke a language that was foreign to him. I watched intently as the scenes depicted Ahmed listening to every word spoken by his new colleagues. As the scenes progressed, an occasional word would be spoken that Ahmed understood. This happened repeatedly until one day, while they were sitting around a campfire, one of the Vikings made an insulting comment about Ahmed's mother, to which he responded in their language, defending his mother's honor. The Vikings were astonished, as was I.

I was only a young boy when I watched this movie. I remember wondering if it were possible to learn a language in such a way - simply being around native speakers, listening closely to their words and trying to understand their meaning from context. Ironically, what I failed to realize at the time is that *is* how I learned my first language.

When I learned English, I first listened to the sounds I heard. I listened a lot. If we consider the fact that most children start speaking between the ages of nine and fourteen months, I probably spent approximately 5,000 waking hours mostly listening. During those months, I experimented with those sounds until I was able to say my first word. As a baby, my mind was a clean slate, completely open to absorb language sounds like a sponge. During the several months that preceded my ability to mimic, the sounds of my native language were being inscribed on my mental "slate." I listened, babbled, and tried desperately to mimic the sounds of my native language until I was eventually able to speak.

During those early years of my life, I was building a

database of language sounds in my mind. By the time I was five, I probably knew about 5,000 words. By 8 years old, I knew around 10,000, and by the time I was an adult, I had a vocabulary of between 20,000 and 30,000 words. Since then, my vocabulary has not stopped increasing.

Because of the immensity of our mental native language database, I believe that most people perceive foreign language sounds through what I call "listening veils." They aren't really perceiving the true sounds at first. They hear them, sure, but only partially.

When our senses intake information, such as foreign language sounds, our minds need to identify what is being perceived. The quickest way for us to identify this information is to check our database to see if we are already familiar with it. This causes us to perceive new information, including sounds, from a biased perspective, constantly comparing new information to old.

This works similarly for all our senses. Imagine seeing an exotic animal for the first time. How would you describe it? The easiest way would be to compare it to another animal that you are familiar with. "It looked kind of like a dog, but with shorter legs, and a snout like a pig." What about describing foods? "It tastes kind of like lemon meringue pie, but milky like vanilla ice cream."

When we listen to a language that we are unfamiliar with, the true sounds of the language are covered by a series of veils which are mere comparisons to known sounds. It takes time to fully unveil the raw sounds of a language as spoken by natives, especially if those sounds differ from our own language sounds. The more times we listen attentively, the more veils are removed, and the closer we can get to hearing the true sounds of the language.

I used to listen to quite a bit of Brazilian music to help me learn Portuguese. One of the words in a song I learned was *razão*, which means reason. However, I was singing the word *ração*, which means ration. The phrase in the song was, "You're the reason I sing," but I was singing, "You're the ration that I sing." I didn't know this until several months after I had "learned" the song, when I was corrected by a Portuguese speaking person.

I had many such experiences in Portuguese. I have confused the word sky with bosom, which was quite embarrassing. During my first trip to Brazil, I had trouble pronouncing the words "nice to meet you." Apparently, I wasn't paying enough attention to the actual sounds of the words.

I remember similar experiences in Spanish, many of them. One word I had trouble with was *ahorita*, which means "right now" in certain Spanish-speaking countries. Since Spanish is spoken rather quickly, I was hearing *arrita*, which isn't even Spanish! I said it this way for several months, without anyone correcting me, until someone finally had the compassion to tell me I was saying it wrong. I couldn't believe it! I unknowingly had been saying it incorrectly for such a long time!

Such occurrences are common among foreigners who are learning English. Take, for example, the word "something." Many foreigners fail to distinguish the "m" sound and mispronounce the word by saying "sonthing." This is due to the fact that they haven't really honed their listening awareness enough to hear the "m" sound in the middle of the stream of sounds that composes the word. Another common mispronunciation of this word is mistaking the "th" sound for the "z" sound, thus producing the word "somezing."

Training your ear on one specific vowel or consonant sound hidden in the midst of several letters is a considerably difficult task. It can be compared to listening to music. Think of any song that has a melody you know. If a certain part of the song that you never focused on was isolated, you probably wouldn't recognize it as part of the song. If you never listened to the bass part before, you wouldn't know what the bass part sounded like. Think of the song again. Do you know how many times the drummer is hitting the high hat in the first measure of the chorus? Is he playing it at all?

It's like this with language as well. When listening to a native speaker say a word or phrase, are you fully aware of how the vowels are being enunciated? How about the intonation? Where is the native speaker placing the tongue? How open is the speaker's throat? Is the sound being directed more out of the nose than the mouth? To what degree is your awareness focused on the sounds being spoken?

So how can we increase our awareness to perceive the true language sounds? This requires saturation - massive exposure to the spoken language, similar to our first experience. In this day and age, it is fairly easy to find audio tracks of almost any widely spoken language. We can use audiobooks, audio course materials, television shows, movies, radio, podcasts, music, and more. The key is to gain access to as many sources as possible, and

subject yourself to those sounds as often as possible.
Turn your car into an immersion machine. Listen to
audiobooks in the foreign language while you're driving.
Listen to audio tracks while working out, cooking,
cleaning, or walking in the park. It's not important that
you understand what is being said at first. It won't take
long before your brain starts to recognize patterns. After
you begin to go through your language courses, you'll
begin to pick out words that you know while listening to
your audio tracks. The main purpose of this type of
exposure is to accustom the ear to the sounds of your
new language.

One important skill to learn is the quieting of the mind
- turning off your mental voice. Instead of biasly
superimposing previously learned sounds over the
incoming unfamiliar sounds, you should listen with a

clean slate, allowing the sounds to paint a sonic mosaic in your mind. Focusing on any certain characteristic of the sound of the native speaker's voice, such as pitch, timbre, or intonation can distract your conscious mind, allowing you to absorb the sounds instead of creating your own version of what you perceive to be the true sounds of the language. Another helpful thing to do while listening to the foreign language, particularly the audios from a language course, is to picture a native speaker saying the words.

I once did an experiment to attempt to recreate a similar experience to my first language learning experience. When I began learning Arabic, I didn't utter a single Arabic word for the first 30 days. I didn't allow myself to be exposed to the written language either. I began an audio course, but without repeating. I also

listened to the spoken language in recorded
conversations, allowing my mind to absorb the sounds.
Nowadays when I speak Arabic, my Arab friends tell me
that I have great pronunciation. I wonder if my
experiment had anything to do with that.

The main point to gather from this perspective on
listening is to listen to the language enough that it
doesn't sound like a foreign language to you anymore.
Again, this will take a substantial amount of time. Don't
let that worry you. There are 24 hours in each day for
every one of us to either use or waste. Language learning
is largely an investment of time, and a highly rewarding
one at that.

04 Mockingbird

Step Two – Mimicry

As I stated previously, **language is something that we initially learn from other people. Why should that change when learning a foreign language?** In my opinion, the term *language fluency* implies that there exists some sort of flow of spoken words between two or more people. After all, a conversation is only possible with two or more parties.

How did you learn to converse or "flow" in your first language? After you began to listen to the spoken language, you desperately strived to produce the words that you heard. You naturally and effectively discovered how to mimic others. Fortunately for you, the people in your life were interested in you learning how to speak, so they coached you; but how were you coached?

Your coaches would make eye contact, speak slowly, and exaggerate the movements of their mouths to show you how to shape the words. This is how you learned to lip read. They would repeat simple words and syllables slowly, giving you the time necessary to try mimicking them. You listened to sounds, watched mouths, and struggled to repeat what you saw and heard. Without this intimate form of coaching, how much harder would it have been to learn your first language?

Most people skip the crucial beginning step of finding native speakers to coach them, and instead buy a language course. Learning a language from a course is kind of like playing catch with yourself. Have you ever tried to get your language course to coach you? I guess it's safe to say that a course can't replace a human being. Regardless of the seemingly endless propaganda served to us by language course companies purporting to offer the quickest and most effective way to learn a language, usually even guaranteed, it's important to realize **that a language course alone will not make you fluent**. Learning to verbally flow in a language with other people will only come by practicing with and being coached by native speakers. Without this key element, most foreign language learners usually either give up, or never become conversationally fluent.

Face to face communication engages multiple senses. When you are learning a new word or phrase during a live conversation, you are having a multisensory experience. Afterwards, your recall of said conversation will be based on the experience you had. It is much easier to remember a word or a phrase that you learned through live coaching than it is to mindlessly memorize words and definitions. The more parts of your awareness that are engaged when learning something, the easier it is to remember it in the future.

It is important to note that communication is so much more than spoken language, and spoken language is often used to complement what is being communicated nonverbally. Most of the vocabulary you learned early in life was through situational context. Picture this scenario: The mother's face turned red as she clenched her teeth, glared at her son and said, "Don't you dare!" The child nearly panics as he quickly understands that he better not even think about doing whatever it was he was going to do. The key to remember here is that experience is what's important. You probably learned the word *hot* from being burned, and *cold* from feeling something cold. Once again, learning vocabulary from live situations requires you to be in the situation in the first place, and with native speakers.

When involved in a live conversation, you have the opportunity to observe the speaker's mouth, just as you did when you learned to lipread your first language. You're also forced to use what vocabulary you know and improvise in the language. You learn new vocabulary by picking up on situational context and visual clues, as well as body language. The feedback from the native speaker induces learning. Also, you're perceiving the language as it is spoken by natives, in its raw, authentic form.

Conversations are spontaneous, filled with emotions, false starts, body language, facial expressions, and variances in intonation, volume, rate of speech, etc. Almost none of the experiences that you benefit from during live conversation can be experienced with a course. Course materials are merely artificial examples of the language. In contrast, spoken language is seemingly alive.

Native speakers, therefore, need to be your primary source for learning the language. Many people shy away from approaching them. Instead, they spend countless hours studying from their language course. Obviously, they receive positive reinforcement from the progress they are making, such as completing a certain number of levels or milestones, which fosters the idea that they are really learning the language. If you spend most of your language learning time studying from a course and little time with native speakers, you will likely learn the language using your own version of pronunciation, which will probably be incorrect. If you continue to spend a considerable amount of time learning the language on your own, you will inevitably solidify these bad habits. Then, when you do approach native speakers, you certainly won't sound natural. You'll simply be speaking the version of the language that you created. When learning on your own, you don't have the company of a native speaker to correct and coach you. Whereas if you are mimicking and learning from native speakers, you can compare your voice to theirs, making adjustments along the way.

Over the years, I've given language lessons to help me with my research. Of all the students that I've coached, very few were willing to actively seek out native speakers. Those that did so achieved success. Those who didn't simply gave up. I have heard many reasons as to why a language learner doesn't approach natives. Most of them were simply excuses, in my opinion. I have determined that the real issue for most people is fear. What do I say? How do I start a conversation? What if I mess up? What if I can't remember how to say anything? What if they laugh at me?

Again, your best bet is to approach this as a child would. Children, even shy ones, learn how to speak their language. Of course, they have the advantage of necessity. If they don't learn to speak, they may not make it very far in life. As a second language learner, most of the time we don't have the element of necessity when it comes to speaking our new language. For most of us, our new language is a hobby, or perhaps we hope to gain from it somehow in the future. Either way, this fear of approaching natives must be overcome in the beginning. **The purpose of learning a language is to communicate with native speakers. Don't let your purpose become your fear and downfall.**

Even though I am highly passionate about languages, I too face similar fears. Facing those fears is what has helped me achieve success in this field. One major element that has helped me to be brave enough to approach natives is having a small arsenal of phrases at my disposal. The best way to obtain this arsenal is to use an all-audio course.

The important thing to remember when beginning with an audio course is to stay true to your commitment to not learn to read the language until you can flow, at least with a basic conversational vocabulary, and have mastered your pronunciation. Luckily, most audio courses teach conversational phrases. As soon as you learn a few phrases, immediately find native speakers with whom to practice them. Hopefully, the native speakers will provide you with feedback and some coaching. Continue this process while you are going through your audio course. Learn a few phrases, practice with natives, receive feedback, return to your course, practice new phrases with natives, and so on. This is how you will become "kindergarten ready."

These face to face experiences are what will solidify your learning of said phrases. If you mispronounce a word or phrase and are corrected by a native speaker, don't be discouraged. Instead, consider yourself fortunate to have successfully reproduced a similar situation to the many that you had in your native language as a toddler. In Italian there is a phrase, *sbagliando s'impara*, which means you learn by making mistakes.

Unfortunately, at least in the United States, by way of politics and old mindsets that refuse to perish, most immigrants to our country are discriminated against and looked down upon. As a language learner, you can consider this as an advantage to you. When a native of this country approaches a foreigner or immigrant and is interested in learning their language, it is a sign of embracing them and their culture. Therefore, most non-U.S. natives welcome this type of interaction. Through your interest in them and their language, which is ultimately intertwined with their culture, they are being validated. They will most likely be delighted by the fact that you approached them and be more than willing to talk with you. Assume and remember this every time fear tries to stop you from approaching.

Forging friendships with native speakers will motivate you to keep going, especially if you know you will see the person or persons again soon. Desire to learn can further the development of your new friendship by causing you to want to meet more often, and by doing so, you become more exposed to the language which helps you learn faster. It is a perpetual cycle of bonding and learning. Each time you speak to a person, you make a personal connection with them, and the experience of each conversation is recorded in your memory. It may take some work to hone your recollection skills, but with practice, you can remember the gist of most real conversations you've ever had with anyone. The most meaningful ones are easier to remember, while the more mundane would require a reminder of what was spoken.

If you are fortunate to live in area in which it is easy to find native speakers of the language you are learning, you should strive to have as much in-person contact with them as possible. If you have difficulty finding native speakers in your community, the world is still at your fingertips via the internet. There are many language exchange websites and mobile apps available. Language exchange can help take away some of the fear as well, since it will be a reciprocal relationship. Both you and the native speaker will be going through a similar process of being coached and corrected. It is important to inform your language exchange partner, however, of your commitment to forgo reading and writing the new language until you have mastered your pronunciation and basic conversational skills. For this reason, you should suggest that the language lessons be done by video or audio chat. Video is best, as it is very similar to in-person communication.

When searching for native speakers to practice with, you may be tempted to practice with bilinguals. They may have moved here later in life and learned English as a second language. They may be children of immigrants and have grown up in the U.S. You may even find people who learned your new language as their second language. It's important to understand with which of these groups you need to practice.

If a person grew up in another country and moved to the U.S. as an adult, it's ok to practice with them. Their native language was probably not affected by them learning English. However, if they moved here as a child, or were born here, do not practice with them until you have become fluent. This is because they are most likely making many grammatical mistakes due to thinking mostly in English. A good way to test this is if they "code-switch" or switch back and forth between both languages frequently when speaking. If your potential teacher learned English as their native language, be careful about learning from them. Even if they are a master certified interpreter such as myself, they still probably possess some flaws in the foreign language.

For me, it's harder to speak a foreign language with someone who speaks English. Even though they are bilingual, part of me knows that the easiest thing for me to do would be to speak English. It's human nature to take the path of least resistance, and since language is birthed out of the need to communicate, that need is most easily satisfied by speaking English with them. Therefore, I always try to find native speakers that know little or no English.

Pride will often try to impede your learning. When native speakers are talking with you and they say something you don't understand, you may be tempted to pretend that you did understand so as not to face embarrassment. This will not benefit you at all. It's ok to ask them to repeat what they said or to slow down. Remember, you are learning.

One very damaging mistake I see language learners make is trying to interpret what is being said to them into English. This will only hinder their learning. First of all, the person speaking already knows what they said to you, so there is no need to interpret for them. Secondly, your goal is to be able to think in the foreign language as well, which can't be done if you keep transforming what you hear into English. When someone talks to you in the foreign language, and you're unsure if you've understood what was spoken, try to repeat it for them in the same language. For example, if they say, "Are you hungry?" you can respond, "Am I hungry?" or simply repeat exactly what they said.

Another potential downfall is the frustration that comes with not understanding words spoken by natives. This will happen more and more often as you surround yourself with them. Remember, the same thing occurred to you in your first language, and it happened for several years. Luckily for you, the stress of not understanding will help you to listen more closely. As you dive into the deep ocean of endless language sounds spoken by natives, your awareness will increase, causing you to try to swim instead of sink, so to speak.

It may take some experimenting with different audio courses before you find one that you feel is right for you. In my opinion, the courses that are most effective are those that prompt the student to recall and speak words that have been previously learned. Following the prompts, there is enough space for the learner to give the answers aloud, followed by a recording of the correct answer given by the native speaker. There are courses that have the student repeat words and phrases after the native speaker, in hopes that they will learn the material from this incessant repetition. Repeating what you hear is not as effective as being prompted to recall what you have already learned. You do initially have to repeat or mimic words when you are first learning them, but repetition alone does not cause learning to take place.

Your audio course must be conversational and simulate interactivity with native speakers. You must be prompted to participate in mock conversations. If the course has dialogues, listen to them often. Try to shadow the conversations to help you build fluency. Shadowing is when you repeat speech immediately after hearing it. If you're shadowing a conversation, for example, you would be speaking the words of the conversation along with the recording, except you will be lagging a little behind the speakers. This will help you build speed and fluidity, train your ear to listen, improve your grammar, solidify learned vocabulary, adopt intonation and pronunciation, develop rhythm, and ultimately help you sound more like a native.

When learning and practicing phrases or shadowing

conversations, imagine yourself talking to natives. Be creative. Imagine your senses being engaged. For example, if the mock conversation is taking place in a coffee shop, imagine being there, smelling the coffee grounds in the air, listening to the music play over the speakers. Include as many senses as possible.

While going through this process of using an audio course to feed your conversational arsenal, don't forget to continue your daily listening practice that was discussed in the previous chapter. Continuous exposure to the spoken language will accelerate your learning at an exponential rate.

Hopefully by this point you have developed enough understanding and courage to face the challenge of learning a new language head-on. Perhaps you still have some doubts about your abilities. I invite you to continue along this journey with me. We are just getting

started.

05 The Sounds of Language

Step Three – Mastering Your Pronunciation

Mastering your pronunciation might be the most important milestone in your journey to learn a foreign language, because at that point, you will have successfully trained your ears to hear the true sounds of the language as spoken by native speakers, and your speech organs to reproduce them. Until you reach that point, how much will you be able to understand when exposed to the spoken language?

Pronunciation is the key element that connects

listening and speaking a language. If you can pronounce a word correctly, then you can hear it correctly. For example, if you think the verb *to be* in Spanish is *estar* (pronounced with an American accent, finishing the word how Americans say the word *star*) then it's no wonder you have limited comprehension of the spoken language. You probably wouldn't be able to recognize the word *estar* in the middle of - *Me dijeron que tengo que estar en la oficina a las ocho en punto.* - because the words you hear in your mind sound different when pronounced by natives. After all, if it doesn't sound like Spanish, is it really Spanish?

Due to the abundance of second language learners that never master their pronunciation, a myth has been embedded into the minds of most people that doing so is unattainable. Hopefully you read the introduction to this book and agreed with me that your human body and mind are similar to those of people from other countries, and you are fully capable of learning to use your speech organs to produce human language sounds, regardless of the language. If you are not convinced of that, please read the introduction again.

Not only is mastering your pronunciation attainable, it is also necessary. One characteristic of a language is that if two or more native speakers of the same language are engaged in verbal conversation, they sound like they are speaking the same language. If they are from Japan and are speaking Japanese, they sound like they are speaking Japanese, using Japanese language sounds, with native-like pronunciation. If it doesn't sound like Japanese, is it really Japanese?

If you are determined to really learn a language, then

all your preconceived doubts with regards to your ability to master your pronunciation need to be dispelled. Whenever those doubts creep up in your mind, remind yourself that you are human, with a similar anatomy to that of a native speaker of the language you are learning. Also remember that the only reason that most of the people you know are not bilingual is simply the approach to language learning that was sold to them.

Up to this point in the book, we have mainly been discussing how to put yourself into a process that is similar to the way you learned your first language. First you listened. Then you learned to mimic native speakers. With coaching you gradually learned how to sound like a native speaker. **The key to learning another language will be to allow your amazing mind and body to naturally learn how to speak from native speakers,**

just like you did once before. Your brain was already programmed as a child to be able to learn language. However, some may still find it difficult to produce the sounds of the language that they are learning. If so, the problems will mostly be awareness issues. In the words of one of my interpreter colleagues, Ron Vasquez, who moved to the U.S. as an adult and learned English without an accent, "It's all about paying attention." It will take some time for you to master your pronunciation, just as it takes children time to no longer sound like toddlers when they speak. Remember that you also once sounded like a toddler in your native language.

At the beginning of your language journey, you need to adopt the mindset that the language you are learning is in fact foreign, and therefore must contain mostly language sounds that you haven't learned to produce yet. Don't expect the sounds to be like those of your first language. If you do happen to discover sounds that are like those of your native language, then simply consider yourself fortunate to not have to struggle with said sounds. All other sounds are foreign, or unknown to you, and should be approached as such.

The skills that you learned in chapter three, "Clean Slate", need to be applied daily. Quiet your mind, and simply observe. Try not to compare what you hear with known sounds. Pretend that your brain is recording the new sounds for later playback. If listening to a recording of a native speaker's voice, try and picture the way they are moving their mouth. If you are face to face with a native, watch their mouth intently.

There are many things to pay attention to when

observing a native speaker talk. First of all, pay attention

to the vowel sounds. In English, our vowels are quite

unstable. Just look at the letter "a" in this paragraph.

How many different versions of "a" sounds can you

find? Fortunately, in many other languages, the vowel

sounds are constant, or at least change very little. When

observing, ask yourself the following questions: Are the

vowels being produced with an open and relaxed throat,

or tight and restricted? Are the vowels being produced

with the speaker's tongue raised in the front or back of

the mouth, or is it flat? Is the sound being produced with

a lot of air flow? Does it sound raspy by friction being

produced in the back of mouth? Do the sounds seem to

be coming more out of the nose, producing a nasal

sound, or is the sound mostly directed out of the mouth?

Does it seem like the tongue is being depressed, forcing

the throat to be exaggeratedly opened, such as with some sounds in Arabic? Are the vowel sounds being produced by opening and closing the jaw, and or changing the shape of the lips, or is the jaw fixed in one position? Are the consonant sounds being produced with the lips, tongue, or teeth? If they are being produced with the lips, does it sound like the lips are loose, allowing a lot of air flow, or are they tight, and pressed together firmly to create the sound? If the consonant sounds are produced with the tongue, where is the tongue being placed? Is it relaxed or is it being pressed firmly against the back side of the upper row of teeth? Are the sounds being produced by the tongue touching some part of the front or the back of the mouth? Is the sound produced by making a buzzing sound? Is there a trill or a flicking of the tongue involved? Do you hear any glottal stops (obstructions of airflow in the vocal cords)?

That may seem like a lot to pay attention to, because it is. Language is quite complex, as are we as human beings. Just always remember that the native speaker's mouth is a human mouth, like the one which you possess. If they are physically able to produce those sounds, then you can learn how to do so as well. Fortunately for you, you're the one who controls what you say and how you say it. When you speak, the sounds that come out of your mouth are programmed by you. You hear those sounds in your mind, then reproduce them with your speech organs. You probably rarely ever catch yourself accidentally speaking your native language with a foreign accent. You speak it like a native speaker. Likewise, when you speak a foreign language, you control how you sound.

Another thing you need to be aware of is that your accent is adaptable, even in your own language. If you were to move to New York, after some time, wouldn't you adopt a New York accent, even if it were slight? What if you were to move to the South? Wouldn't you eventually adopt perhaps a bit of a southern accent? It is likely that you would. Even if you don't think so, close family and friends often pick up on the changes when you come back home to visit. As humans, we adapt to our environment. Being exposed to speakers from a certain region causes us to adapt to the way they speak. Likewise, constant exposure to native speakers of a language will have the same effect. Trust your abilities, as hopefully by now you understand that you are a language learning machine.

There are some mental tricks that you can employ

when working on your pronunciation. One thing you can do is speak English but impersonate a foreign accent. It's just like trying to sound like Arnold Schwarzenegger, Speedy Gonzales, or Pepé Le Pew. Another good technique is to try to match the pitch of the native speaker's voice as closely as you can. If the speaker is a member of the opposite sex, simply adjust the octave of your voice to match their pitch, either one octave lower or higher. Also, pay close attention to intonation. If a word or phrase rises or falls, or a certain part of a word is emphasized, mimic it exactly.

Speed is also a very important factor when it comes to flowing. The difficulty with language speed is that in the beginning, your speech organs are not used to producing the language sounds. Therefore, you will have to speak slower than a native at first. It's important not to rush your rate of speech if it means sacrificing your pronunciation. Speak slowly enough to say each word perfectly. Muscle memory will work to your advantage, and after enough slow practice, speed will come naturally. When you're by yourself, practice saying words that are difficult for you. Analyze each sound of the word. When you realize which part of the word or word combinations are causing you trouble, pronounce the difficult sounds repeatedly like an exercise. Train your speech organs to sound the way you want them to.

Go ahead and accept the fact that this process will be a challenge and may take longer than you want it to. It's simply a matter of persistence coupled with self-critique. The only real way to prove to yourself that you are kindergarten ready in a foreign language is by recording your own voice and truly observing yourself speaking with great pronunciation. You must record yourself regularly until you have reached the point at which you can honestly say that you have mastered your pronunciation.

06 Personal Experience

Once you have mastered your pronunciation and have become conversationally proficient, at least on a basic level, your next step is to learn how to read and write in the foreign language. The most effective way of doing this is to use different types of language courses. Yes, I really did just recommend the use of language courses! As I stated previously, most language courses are not wrong in their approach, rather they are misplaced. However, once you have established the basic conversational skills in a language, and have mastered your pronunciation, language courses can be highly effective.

Before diving into how to find the right set of language courses for yourself, I would like to share some of my personal experiences that helped me to develop into the language learner that I am today. My understanding of both the effectiveness and ineffectiveness of language courses developed after I had become proficient in learning foreign languages. I became fluent in two foreign languages well before I ever found a language course that worked for me.

Prior to my first trip to Brazil, I was unable to find a decent Portuguese course. Before I left the U.S., my dad gave me a pocket-sized dictionary filled with Portuguese words that I couldn't read. When I boarded the plane, I was delighted to find a large group of Brazilian passengers that were returning to their country. I immediately began to interact with them in hopes that I would be able to learn some words before we arrived in Brazil. And so began my first foreign language learning experience.

Once we landed in Brazil, I immediately went to the airport bookstore in search of something that could help me learn. All I could find were some bilingual dictionaries and a small phrasebook. I purchased the phrasebook and started fumbling through it. I couldn't read any of the Portuguese, and I knew that if I tried, I certainly wouldn't know how to pronounce the words. At that moment an idea occurred to me. I was surrounded by native speakers. Why not have them teach me?

At the time, I had a horrible cough from almost drowning at the beach shortly before my trip. I wanted the people I met and interacted with to know that I wasn't sick, so they wouldn't be wary of speaking with me. I searched in the phrasebook to find the health section, approached the next Brazilian person that I saw, and had them coach me. I pointed to the words and phrases in the book that I wanted to learn, and made gestures hoping that the person would understand that I wanted to learn how to say the indicated word or phrase. After learning the basic greeting phrases, the next thing I learned how to say in Portuguese was, *"I'm not sick. I have water in my lungs."* At last, I had something useful to say! Every time I coughed, if a person gave me the "please don't get me sick" face, I would use that same phrase.

I literally used and abused that phrasebook and my pocket dictionary during my trip. I didn't try to figure out how to read anything at that point, because I knew I wouldn't pronounce it correctly. I would simply find someone to talk to, think of a topic, find that topic in the phrase book, and point to the words I wanted to learn. I would listen intently as the native speakers coached me, watching their mouths shape the words, trying to match their pitch, intonation, accent, and pronunciation the best I could. After I learned a phrase or two from one person, I would immediately go and practice what I learned with someone else. I would practice the same phrases with as many different Brazilians as possible. I had a great advantage, too. There were Brazilians everywhere.

After just three days of being in Brazil. I was able to hold long conversations with native speakers about a variety of topics. Most of the people complimented me, telling me that I spoke with barely any accent. When I returned to the U.S., I decided to continue learning Portuguese. I just happened to live in a town where several Brazilians resided, so they became my new best friends. I made phone calls as often as possible to my friends in Brazil and learned how to read and write by exchanging emails and utilizing online chat rooms. I searched constantly in book stores for Portuguese courses that would help to further my learning. I found some that I liked, but most of them were ineffective.

Later that year I began working at the turkey plant and decided to learn Spanish. Since I had figured out a way to effectively learn Portuguese, I simply repeated the process in Spanish. During my first day on the job, I was fortunate enough to have someone teach me the most useful phrases that I could have learned: *"How do you say __?"* and *"What's this called?"* I purchased a phrasebook and a dictionary and did exactly what I had done in Brazil. I spent the entire time on the job learning words and phrases from natives. I became close friends with several of my coworkers and would spend plenty of time with them outside of work. This time, the process worked much quicker. I became fluent in just three short months.

After I became fluent in Spanish, I decided to start learning some phrases from the other migrant workers at the turkey plant, most of which were Chinese. I did the logical thing. I purchased a phrasebook and began hanging out with the Chinese workers. Unfortunately, the only real time I had to spend with them was when our lunch breaks coincided, since we worked in different departments. Nevertheless, I was able to learn a lot of useful phrases in Mandarin. The few phrases that I learned in Korean and in the Mayan language called Mam, were from a smattering of conversations that I would have with native speakers.

At one point, I decided to learn French. I went to the bookstore several times, and purchased several courses, but I had no access to native speakers. I spent several months trying to learn French before I gave up for the time being. My pronunciation was horrible, and I didn't feel like I was making any progress at all. I did the same thing with a few other languages, such as Hebrew and Greek, yet with little to no success.

One night, while I was desperately rummaging the shelves of my beloved book store, hoping to find the diamond in the rough, an old man who was in the same aisle picked up a language course and asked me if I had tried it. I replied that I hadn't. He then began bragging that with that same language course, he had learned how to pick up women in five different languages. After I laughed, I took a look at the course and decided to purchase the French version of it. When I got in my car, I opened the course up and was surprised to find that it was only a set of tapes. There was neither a dictionary nor a course book. I was a little disappointed but popped one of the tapes into my tape deck anyway.

Throughout the lessons, I was being instructed to listen to the voice of the native speaker on the recording, and prompted to participate in mock conversations, paying close attention to my pronunciation. Surprisingly, this method proved to be quite effective. Using an all audio course was the closest thing I had experienced to speaking with native speakers. I learned more French over the next few days than I had during the six months that I had spent trying to learn with books. I gave up on French again shortly afterwards, since I didn't have access to any native speakers. This was before the days of high-speed Internet, smartphones, and video chat.

Later that year, I was invited to take a trip to Europe. Our group would be going to Switzerland and Italy. I did some research and found out that six or more different languages were spoken in the two countries we were going to visit. I immediately returned to the bookstore to purchase all-audio courses in those particular languages, but was only able to find them in German, Swiss German, Mandarin, and Italian.

A few months before our trip, it just so happened that the Italian interpreter for our group was not going to be able to join us, so I was asked to learn Italian. I didn't know if I could learn it in time to be of service on the trip, but I decided to try anyway. Almost immediately after I decided to do so, I had a very fortunate experience. I was working in the local mall at the time. One day, a teenage boy came into the store that could barely speak English. He said that he was from Italy and that he was in the U.S. visiting his uncle who owned the pizza restaurant at the mall. I immediately began to frequent the pizza restaurant every day and practiced Italian with the restaurant owner and his nephew. Once in Europe, I was thrilled to find native speakers of Spanish, Portuguese, French, German, Swiss German, Mandarin, Japanese, and Italian. I was in a language lover's paradise. By the time we got to Italy, I had learned enough Italian that we didn't have any communication problems during our trip.

It was on that trip that I decided that I wanted to spend the rest of my life learning languages. I met several people who were fluent in five or more languages and began to believe that I could become like them. After returning to the U.S., I planned another trip back to Europe, but only to Italy. I spent the next three months studying Italian and practicing with the owner of the pizza restaurant. Once back in Italy, I enrolled in a daily Italian class, which lasted about five hours each day. I quickly began to thrive in the Italian language. After just six weeks of being there, I had become more fluent in Italian than I was in Spanish. I had finally become fluent in my fourth language.

Since that time, I have actively sought out language courses that would help me learn the languages of native speakers with which I maintained regular contact. When

I was working in the mall, I had access to people from Israel, Pakistan, Vietnam, China, and Taiwan. I bought several different types of courses, but the ones that were most effective to start out with were audio courses. Additionally, the only success I ever had in any language came from practicing what I learned in the courses with native speakers.

I once spent two years studying Syrian Arabic with a course, yet with no access to native speakers. Once I moved to the city I live in now, I met several native speakers of that dialect of Arabic and found that my Arabic language skills were very limited. I struggled with even the most basic conversations. I only became proficient after having spent a sufficient amount of time with Arabs from that region of the Middle East.

I finally had success in French after having moved into

an apartment a few doors down from a native speaker. Through daily practice with him and his family, along with the language courses I was using, I was able to become quite proficient in the language.

The reason I wanted to explain this much of my personal experience is to show you that my perspective on language courses is that of a person who learned how to become fluent in foreign languages with and without the use of language courses. I have been an avid language learner since 2001 and have purchased a plethora of different types of courses. I have seen and even bought into the advertisements claiming that their way is the best way, or their method is the fastest way to learn a language. I've found a few courses that I like, and many that I hate. Had I approached language learning the way most people do, by purchasing the language course with the most convincing advertisement without going through the experiences that I mentioned in this chapter, I doubt I would be fluent in anything other than English.

My goal now is to help you to dissolve the misconceptions that you have been led to believe, as well as open your eyes to the reality of learning languages with the aid of courses. By uncovering the myths behind most language course advertisements, you will be better prepared to search for the right set of language courses for you.

07 Of Course

Step 4 - Learning to Read, Write, and the Basics of Grammar

The most common myth I see advertised is that a certain course will make you fluent in just a few months. First of all, like I've stated several times in this book already, a language course alone will not make you fluent. Secondly, the math needs to be understood. Most adults know 20,000 - 30,000 words or more in their native language. Most 8-year-olds know about 10,000 words, and the average kindergartener knows around

5,000. If we were to label these three levels as basic, moderate, and native-like fluency, the following would be a more accurate timeline for achieving each level of fluency:

Basic Fluency - 5,000 words

10 words per day = 500 days ~ 17 months

20 words per day = 250 days ~ 9 months

Moderate Fluency - 10,000 words

10 words per day = 1,000 days ~ 34 months

20 words per day = 500 days ~ 17 months

Native-Like Fluency - 20,000 to 30,000 words

10 words per day = approximately 7 years

20 words per day = approximately 3.5 years

In other words, how can you expect to become fluent in a short amount of time from a course? It is virtually impossible. Just as vitamins are strictly supplements and cannot replace food, language courses, too, are supplemental in nature. The quickest way you can learn a language is to have massive exposure to native speakers.

One common buzz word in the language learning genre is immersion. Courses that claim to be full immersion are falsifying their claims. You can't immerse yourself in a culture in front of your computer or on a mobile app. That's sort of I like trying to get a tan by watching a video of a sunset.

As far as "point and click" courses are concerned, I have found them to be minimally effective, unless used for passive learning. It can be compared to a multiple-choice exam that a student would take in school. When I was a kid, I always hoped that our teacher would give us this type of exams. This is because when you are presented with a number of possible answers, all you have to do is use process of elimination and single out the correct answer. You don't even have to know what the correct answer is. You simply need to know what the wrong answers are. On the other hand, on a test in which you are asked to fill in the correct answer, with no answers to choose from, you either know the information or you don't. While engaged in conversation with native speakers, the learner does not get to choose what they need to say from a list of possible answers. They need to recall what they have learned, or not communicate effectively. In real life, you must have easy access to your learned vocabulary and expressions.

Learning by repetition has the same downfall. Being

able to repeat what you hear is an invaluable skill, however, little to no recall is required. The most effective form of repetition is repeating the action of recalling learned information, which will reinforce what has been learned. As I stated in chapter four, an ideal course is one that teaches you how to say something, later prompts you to recall said word or phrase, then gives you the correct answer to compare with your own.

Many language courses as well as foreign language classroom curriculums focus way too much on grammar in the beginning. Picture the following scenario; Imagine that your wedding anniversary is coming up, and you would like to do something special for your spouse. You decide to take some guitar lessons and learn how to play him or her a song on that upcoming special day. During the first guitar lesson, you explain your intentions to the instructor, and tell him the name of the song you wish to learn. Instead of teaching you how to play anything, the instructor teaches you all the different parts of the guitar. This process takes up the entire lesson, and you leave fairly disappointed and confused.

The next week, you return in hopes that you might learn to play at least one or two chords, so that you can begin practicing the song. Upon arriving to the lesson, the instructor tests you on your knowledge of the parts of the guitar. Since this wasn't the reason you began guitar lessons in the first place, you hadn't studied what you learned in your first lesson, and you failed his test. In response to your poor performance on the test, the instructor repeats the first lesson, explaining more thoroughly each detail about each part of the guitar.

How many more lessons would you attend before

deciding to either quit or find a different instructor? This may seem silly, but many people approach language learning in a similar way, especially in the classroom setting, by mainly focusing on grammar. The problem is that grammar is only part of that which language consists of. To attempt to learn a language by focusing mostly on grammar is almost like trying to heat a cup of water by learning about the parts of a microwave or learning about electrical engineering when all you want to do is turn your television on.

In my opinion, the best way to approach grammar is to not worry about it for a while. Focusing mainly on grammar rules in the beginning of one's language learning journey can be an arduous chore, a boring one at that, and certainly doesn't provide much mental stimulation other than stress and frustration. If you have been learning your new language based on the philosophy of this book up to this point, then you are simulating your first language learning experience. Grammar is something that you began to focus on after you had become conversationally proficient in your native language. It was not taught to you as a way to learn how to become fluent, rather it was a method of refining and furthering your understanding of your mother tongue.

In the beginning, grammar is best absorbed by learning how to speak like a native, provided you pay attention to sentence structure. By learning the language as it is spoken by natives, your brain will naturally put the pieces of the grammar puzzle together. This is one reason why shadowing the spoken language regularly is so helpful. When studying grammar after one has gained a decent grasp on the language, it serves to be a much more rewarding process, allowing the learner to reveal previously unsolved mysteries and answer unasked questions about the language. For these reasons, I recommend you don't use any grammar-based workbooks until after you feel comfortable with the language.

A great idea is to find courses and/or apps that include videos of native speakers speaking the words and phrases that you are learning. This will help you to see how to form the words and therefore enhance your pronunciation. This is highly effective, as it induces the learning of lip reading. When you lipread you are watching someone's mouth formulate words, and you can mentally hear those words in your mind. In my experience, up-close videos of natives speaking have been the most effective tool for learning at home.

Monolingual courses have also proven to be very effective for me. By monolingual, I mean that the course has no English script nor audio. You can usually find these by chasing the advertisements for full immersion, even though you can be sure that it isn't true immersion. Nevertheless, going through a course with no script or audio in English can help you to think and reason in the language you are learning. It is also a great way to absorb grammar rules by context. Also, any language learning software or app you use should have a voice recognition component so that you can compare your recorded voice with that of the native speaker's.

Avoid courses with transliteration. Transliteration is when the pronunciation is spelled out in English letters next to or underneath the foreign language. This simply causes you to compare the foreign language sounds to English language sounds. It is only a hindrance to your pronunciation.

Hopefully by now you have gained some perspective on how to find the right courses for you. I pluralize the word courses, because I believe that you will need to use more than one. All courses are different, and sometimes what is considered basic in one course isn't introduced until the more advanced levels in another. Using only one language course will leave you with many gaps in your vocabulary. In my opinion, it's important to see the courses as a way of understanding about 70 percent of the words that are spoken on a daily basis. The rest you can learn by massive exposure to both the spoken and written language, as well as learning by context. In my experience, in order to reach this 70 percent comprehension level, I usually need at least one audio course, one or two mobile apps or software, with at least one of them being monolingual, as well as a set of beginner to advanced course books.

One thing I had to learn the hard way was the need to master course materials. When I was just starting out, my goal was to finish a course as quickly as possible with the mindset that the sooner I finished the course, the sooner I would become fluent. This caused me to not absorb enough of the information and therefore was counterproductive. Repeated exposure is the way to master the material. Take your time with each lesson. Go through each lesson over and over until you feel you have it mastered. You should know it so well that it even seems tedious to review. Periodically I will still review course material that I have previously mastered. As far as the audio portions are concerned, I listen to the tracks so much that I can anticipate the next word or phrase to be uttered.

Another tip is to only study for 30 minutes at a time. Afterwards, take a 10-15-minute break to allow your subconscious to process the material to which it was exposed. For some people, 30 minutes a day is all they can handle. After about 30 minutes, your brain will absorb less and less information as time goes on. Some courses even recommend only studying for 30 minutes a day, but when I think about how many hours per day a student spends learning at school, I believe the average human mind is more than capable of studying for an extended period of time, provided the person takes adequate breaks every 30 minutes.

This chapter is my long answer to the question that

many people have asked me over the years. Which is the best language course to become fluent? The answer is none. Courses are only a small part of the immense task of really learning a language.

08 Fluency

I've always been fascinated by spy movies, particularly when it comes to the spies' foreign language skills. Most of the time the character speaks a foreign language with seeming fluency and virtually no accent, so as to pass as a native. Another term for this level is *native-like fluency*. That level of mastery has always intrigued me. I used to wonder what it would be like to become so fluent in a language that I could pass as a native.

To attain such a high level of fluency may be a lofty goal for you, and depending on what your language learning goals are, it might even be out of the question. Either way, if you've reached this point in the book, I can only assume that you at least desire to become fluent in a foreign language. But what does the term *fluent* really mean? At what level can one claim to be fluent in a language? In my opinion, it is a highly misunderstood and often misused term. Many people claim to be fluent in a language yet struggle with their pronunciation, or even struggle holding basic conversations.

The concept of being fluent is usually understood to mean that a person has reached THE level of proficiency called fluency, as if fluency were a destination. However, fluency is neither a level nor a point in a language learner's journey. It is more like a never-ending staircase on which each step is a higher degree of ability to flow in conversation with natives as well as a higher level of comprehension and usage of both the spoken and written language. The first step on this staircase is the point at which a language learner has become proficient in conversation and has mastered their pronunciation. Regardless of their limited vocabulary, this person can verbally flow in conversation.

Just like children are considered fluent, even on a basic level before they start kindergarten, so too can the language learner be considered fluent at this level. Herein lies the problem. Obviously by this point the learner hasn't learned to read or write and has a very basic understanding of grammar. If you compare this person's level of proficiency to someone who has mastered a language, then the term fluent, even though it applies to both people, is rather vague.

If you have followed the steps described in the first

seven chapters of this book, having built up your listening skills, learned how to mimic, mastered your pronunciation, learned to read and write as well as the basics of grammar with a few different types of courses, then chances are you are fluent to a degree. You possess basic language skills, yet continuously find yourself not understanding many things that you read or hear. You can impress your friends and survive in day to day conversations, but your vocabulary still seems limited, and your ability to express yourself is still underdeveloped.

So, what do you need to do in order to climb up to the next step on the ladder of fluency? If you bought into my philosophy that completing the steps described thus far will help you to understand about 70 percent of what you read and hear daily, then the first logical thing would be to build your vocabulary. In the next chapter, we will discuss many ways to rapidly and effectively build your vocabulary. Also, you should realize that your understanding of grammar is probably still limited at this point. We will work on that too. Before getting into those advanced concepts, there are some things that you can do mentally to prepare yourself for the next level. The first thing to do is to pay attention to the way you express yourself in the foreign language. When you reach a certain degree of proficiency, you will find yourself being able to flow in conversation with ease, but you may be structuring your sentences as you do in your own language. Even if you use proper grammar, you will be mostly translating from English into the new language. For example, "Call me back." In Spanish, you don't say, "Call me back." Instead, you say, "Return my call" or just "Call me." "Leave me alone," is also not used. It doesn't make sense. They say, "Leave me in peace," which sounds funny to an English speaker. You must learn how the natives speak. You can't just look up words in a dictionary and translate in order to speak like a native. Your vocabulary, including expressions, has to come from observation and comprehension of the foreign language as it is being used, either from interaction with native speakers, literature written in the foreign country, or media originating from there. Be honest with yourself about the expressions and sentence structure that you use. Are you saying something that you translated from your own language, or are you repeating what you've observed as being an actual expression?

The next thing that I'm about to tell you might seem odd if you haven't experienced it, but becoming multilingual is almost like creating multiple personalities. It sounds strange but ask any polyglot, and they will more than likely tell you the same thing. To become fluent in another language, you have to create a new version of yourself. When speaking another language, I feel like I am a person from a different country. When I speak Spanish, I become Mexican. I'm Brazilian when I speak Portuguese. I genuinely feel and think differently. My body language and mannerisms change. Maybe this happened naturally but I am still aware of the thought process that takes place. You need to picture yourself as being a native speaker. If you're learning Italian, picture yourself as an Italian. Picture yourself in Italy conversing with another Italian. Visualize it vividly. Involve your senses. Picture yourself speaking just like they do.

Once, I had an enlightening experience with a polyglot taxi driver. When my wife and I got into his vehicle, I noticed he was from the Middle East. We engaged in conversation and he mentioned to me that he speaks several languages. I then began to talk to him in the different languages that I knew at the time. He was good and didn't have any problem answering me in each language that I spoke, except for Hebrew. After a few minutes, he looked at my wife and said, "Wow. When your husband speaks these languages, he speaks each one as if it were his own language." It was at that point that I realized that I truly do adopt each new language as my own. They become a part of me and who I am. Adopt this mindset, as crazy as it sounds, and you will have success on your language journey.

As your fluency builds, the more natural it will seem

to speak like a native. When a word or phrase surfaces in your mind, you should be able to spontaneously spurt it out as a native would. Everything you have learned should come out as a reflex triggered by an emotion or thought, just like the spontaneous speech of your native tongue. Adopt each word and phrase as your own, making it a part of who you are and how you express yourself.

One of the first signs that I am becoming fluent in a language is when I start dreaming in it. It's always an exciting experience, and whenever I start learning a new language, I expectantly await the morning that I will wake up after having had one of these magical experiences. Another sign is when I find myself naturally thinking to myself in the foreign language. Rather than simply working out words and phrases in my mind, I'm having a conversation with myself, just as I would in English.

You can train yourself to think in the foreign language. Again, it may sound silly, but you should make up characters in your mind with whom to speak. Have mental conversations with these native-speaking characters in their language. I do this all the time, and with little to no effort. In fact, a large part of my day is spent speaking with these imaginary characters, provided I'm not mentally engaged in something else.

Hopefully the aforementioned mental tricks will help you to achieve different levels of fluency. For some people though, just the idea of becoming fluent can be overwhelming, especially if they desire to achieve a native-like fluency. The best way to attack this apprehension is to think about how long it took you to learn your first language. Verify your level of commitment. If you really want to learn a language, then you should allow yourself as much time as you were allotted as a child. Although, if you follow the steps in this book, the process will be much faster.

To become a certified interpreter, I had to achieve a native-like fluency as a prerequisite even before I began my interpreter training. I began learning Spanish in 2001 and didn't become certified until 2009. I didn't become master certified, which is much more difficult, until 2017. It took me approximately 16 years to master Spanish and my interpreting skills to such a degree that I could receive the label of master certified. Even after having achieved that level, I am still quite limited in my vocabulary when compared to a well-educated native speaker. The Spanish staircase is still seemingly endless for me, and I don't perceive there to be any cap on how much I can learn. Every day new phrases and vocabulary are being added to the language as it evolves. Just like fluency, mastery is not a single level. Both are vast spectrums.

A great thing for you to do, especially if you are only learning your second language, is to have a decent approach to goal setting. Primarily, I like to set my goals based on the courses I am using. These goals are measurable and easily visualized. I focus on short-term as well as long-term goals. For example, I might say, "I will complete this lesson today, this unit this week, this level this month, this entire course this year." Some other goals could be ordering food in a restaurant, having a short conversation with a native, singing a song all the way through, and understanding a telephone conversation or a Facebook post. The point is that you need to be able to gauge your progress. Be reasonable with yourself. This will take time. Always remember, you will only really learn this language if you don't quit.

09 Wordsmith

Step 5 - Building Your Vocabulary

In order to climb the ladder of fluency, you must constantly build your vocabulary. If you have already achieved a vocabulary of a couple thousand words, you are likely able to understand most of the spoken and written language that you are exposed to regularly, yet you are constantly finding words that you don't understand. Such a small percentage of an adult native's known vocabulary is used daily. This doesn't mean that the rest of their vocabulary isn't important. There are over 170,000 words in the English language, yet only about 3,000 words make up around 95 percent of what is used with regularity. When topics arise that are not part of the daily, mundane situations that a person normally encounters, they need to be able to draw upon their passive vocabulary. These are words that every adult native has learned and has mastery over and can draw upon in an instant.

Think about it this way. In your native language, you could probably explain to your neighbor that you need to borrow some jumper cables, because at some point in your life you had an experience which required you to have your car jump started. But when was the last time you had to have such a discussion? Luckily it doesn't come up on a regular basis. The term *jumper cables* is very important to know in case of such an emergency. It's just not a part of your daily, active vocabulary. Do you know how to say *jumper cables* in your new language? If not, then that is what I call a vocabulary hole.

Fluency is often topical, meaning that you have learned the words related to topics that you have had experience with. If you work in a Mexican restaurant and have learned quite a bit of Spanish vocabulary from the workers, then you have no problem talking about subjects related to food and restaurants. Yet as soon as you find yourself in a situation that you have not had experience in, such as having to take your car to a mechanic that only speaks Spanish, your restaurant vocabulary will not help you much.

Frequently when I am engaged in conversation in a

foreign language with someone, or reading a news article, I will come across vocabulary holes. These are missing parts of my vocabulary, which would not be missing in the vocabulary of an adult native speaker. Vocabulary holes are caused by lack of exposure to subject matter in the language. I remember one time at my first interpreting job, which was at an elementary school, I was asked by a teacher to translate a letter that was to be sent home to her students' parents. It was a short letter, so she stood by while I translated. She noticed that I had to look up the word *rabbit* in Spanish. She was surprised, and asked, "You know how to say all this, but you can't say *rabbit*?" I was quite embarrassed, but I told her that if I never had spoken about rabbits with someone, read anything about rabbits, seen any movies about rabbits, and was never otherwise exposed

134

to the word *rabbit* in Spanish, then I would have no

reason to know the word. Fortunately, I now know that

this was a cop-out. I should have done the work and

exposed myself to as much vocabulary as possible on a

regular basis, especially working as an interpreter.

The best way to attack the vocabulary hole obstacle is

head on. Be proactive. Use the techniques described in

chapter three about massive exposure to the spoken

language, with a focus on listening for comprehension.

Do the same thing with the written language. Make sure

your language input is mostly in the foreign language.

You can change your language settings in most

electronic devices. You can do the same thing with your

email and social media accounts. Read news articles

written in countries where the language you are learning

is spoken. Read books and magazines printed in the

same countries. It's important to avoid translated literature as much as possible, until you have reached the point at which you are able to point out translation errors. Always check the source to make sure its origin is a foreign country where your new language is spoken.

If you aim to achieve native-like fluency, you need to broaden the scope of your language exposure. You need massive exposure to all the different registers of the language, in a wide variety of subjects. You need exposure to the news in all possible media including written, audio, and video. Consume novels and biographies both in the traditional format and in audio. Watch talk shows, sitcoms, dramas, and movies. Listen to lyrical music. Devour books or articles about science, history, politics, religion, and any other topic that you can think of. Bring to mind a subject and research it online in the foreign language. Online encyclopedias are sometimes available in foreign languages. Use them.

In order to not become overwhelmed by the amount of vocabulary that you need to learn, it's important to slow down and have as much repeated exposure to the material you are learning from as is necessary. If it's an audiobook, listen to the same chapter repeatedly until you can fully comprehend everything that you hear. If the device you are using to play the audiobook has the ability to skip back in small increments, such as 10 or 30 seconds, then repeat each segment until you understand each word. Try to find the written version of the book to use as a reference as you listen. If the book has been translated into English, procure the English version as well. Just remember that translations can be faulty.

If you're reading an online article, save a copy of it,

and read it as many times as it takes for you to understand every word. If you're watching a movie or a show, repeat each scene or clip as needed. Using subtitles can be helpful as well. I recommend watching without subtitles at first, to judge your level of comprehension and force your brain to attempt to connect the puzzle pieces, absorbing meaning through context. Afterwards, watch with the foreign language subtitles if available. If you watch with English subtitles, you'll more than likely be reading more than listening, which won't help you to learn the words. However, watching with English subtitles can help you get a better sense of the storyline. If you choose to do this, only do it once, and always return to the same movie or show using the previous steps. Your goal should be to watch without the need for subtitles.

I also recommend that you fall in love with music in the language that you are learning. Music affects us on an emotional level. For that reason, the words that you learn from songs will have a deep meaning to you. Additionally, if you like a particular song, you're more likely to listen to it often and memorize the lyrics. Through learning songs, you will absorb a massive amount of vocabulary, grammar, slang, and connect more with the culture. It's fairly easy to find the lyrics of almost any song, so you can take your time to look up the words to fully understand each song. Music videos are great too, since you can watch mouths, and gather some context clues from the scenes.

It's important to understand how to effectively look up words. Most people simply type a word or phrase into an online translator, yet they are unaware of the ineffectiveness of this method. I typed the phrase into an online translator; "I don't really know why she skipped town." I copied and pasted the translation and reversed the language pair to translate it back into English, which resulted in, "It is not known exactly why the city is omitted." When I simplified the phrase to, "She skipped town," the result was, "She jumped the city".

The reason online translators are ineffective is because words can have more than one meaning. Let's look at the word *way*. How many *ways* can we use it?

1. Well, this is one *way*. (form)

2. I'm on the *way*. (path)

3. Show me the *way* to cook pizza. (method)

4. Which *way* did he go? (direction)

5. That's *way* too hot for me. (emphasis)

6. I like the *way* you talk. (manner)

7. By the *way*, (idiom)

There are probably more *ways* than those listed, but you see my point. An online translator doesn't always pick the correct meaning of the word or phrase that you are looking up.

A better way to look up words is to use monolingual dictionaries, as this gets you thinking more in the foreign language. After you have looked up the monolingual definition, look up the bilingual definition using a bilingual dictionary, not a translator. Language forums are very helpful for this, since you can ask other users how to define or translate certain terms. After you look up the bilingual definition, try to find the word or phrase in context. Search the term by itself using a search engine and see what pops up. If you are looking up a noun, use an image search.

One trap I used to find myself constantly falling into is the ambush of false cognates. Some people refer to false cognates as false friends. A cognate is a word that looks similar and may even sound similar in both languages and has the same meaning in each. A false cognate is just like a cognate yet has a different meaning. A hard lesson for me was when a Hispanic coworker told me she was *embarazada,* which means pregnant, not embarrassed. I'll let you use your imagination to feel the awkwardness I endured in that situation. Once you get deep enough into learning your new language, you'll find patterns which indicate that a word is a cognate. Never assume the meaning. Always research the word to be sure. Also, in many languages nouns have genders. Don't automatically assume the noun's gender. Learn the gender as being part of the word.

I'd like to reiterate that repeated exposure is the key. Reading a passage or watching a clip multiple times, although it may seem monotonous, is way more effective than memorizing vocabulary lists or using flash cards. Growing your vocabulary from repeated exposure ensures that you are always learning from context.

Learning a new word and later being able to recall it is like learning a person's name. If you rarely interact with the person after meeting them, the next time you see them it may be difficult to remember their name. But, if you see the person regularly, and interact with them, their name is simply part of who they are. Likewise, if you learn a word, and are exposed to that word often, it will be hard to forget it. After a little while you don't even have to try hard to draw upon the memory of when you learned the word, as it just becomes part of your vocabulary. For example, can you remember the time you learned the word *house*? Me neither. I do, however remember the time I learned the word aesthetic, which rarely comes up in conversation. I remember where I was sitting and with whom I was speaking when they explained what it meant. Whenever I'm exposed to the term now, the memory of when I learned it slightly grazes my consciousness, yet when I use common words such as *house*, I don't experience anything of the sort.

Just as I've described before, using mental tricks can help you to remember words more quickly and easily. One thing you can do is to picture an image of the word in your mind, not the letters of the word, rather the meaning of the word. If you are learning the word *cat* in the foreign language, picture the biggest cat you can imagine. Make your mental image extraordinary and bizarre. Give the cat wings and imagine that cats in the language's country of origin all have wings. Once you have a clear image of the new species of cat you have created, make up a scenario. Perhaps the winged feline is chasing you toward the edge of a cliff. Imagine that you are running away from the creature alongside a native speaker of your new language. Imagine yourself yelling out to him, "What is that?", to which he replies something along the lines of, "That's a cat!" The more bizarre and far-fetched you make the scenario, the easier it will be to remember it. It's important to always include yourself and a native speaker in your mental scenarios. Add as many emotions as you can. Think about how scared you were as you were on the verge of becoming cat food. Be as creative as possible.

Another thing I like to do is have mental replays of

words that I have learned from natives. I mentally relive the situations when I learned the words over and over in my mind. I used to do this on purpose, but now it happens naturally. This may take some work to get into the habit of doing, but it helps a great deal. The key is to spend time on each word as you are learning it. Vocabulary building is not about how many words you can learn quickly. It's about how many words you can effectively recall and use at will.

10 Refinement

Step 6 – Sophistication

In order to achieve native-like fluency, you will need more than just an extensive vocabulary. You will need to reach a level of sophistication similar to that which you have in your native language. Most of the techniques and exercises mentioned in this chapter will be things that would be pretty easy to accomplish in your native language. Let that be your measuring stick throughout this process. When you face difficulty in performing these exercises, just remember how easy it would be to do the same in your native language. This analysis will also help you to measure your progress in the foreign language that you are learning.

In the chapter about courses, I recommended not to use grammar-based workbooks until you have reached a certain level of fluency. If at this point you feel like you are ready, then you should do the following: Purchase a few or even several different bilingual grammar workbooks until you find those that are effective for you. Go through them slowly and repeat each lesson until you have it mastered. You will also need to set up some sort of review schedule so that you don't forget what you've learned.

When you get to the unavoidable sections on verb conjugation, don't let them scare you away. In conversations I've had over the years with language learners, one of the biggest difficulties most people face is the concept of verb conjugations. Unfortunately, verb conjugations are usually taught early on in schools and courses, which tends to overwhelm the student who hasn't even reached the most basic level of fluency. While learning about verbs and their seemingly endless conjugations, it's wise to use mental scenarios as well. You can start by thinking about the scenarios in your native language. Pick any simple scenario you want, such as going to the grocery store to buy some juice.

Picture a timeline, like an arrow on a chalkboard. If now is the present, then you can talk about now in terms of, "I'm buying juice." If it's something you are going to do, it's "I'm going to buy some juice." If it already happened, then obviously it's, "I bought juice." If you picture these three events on a timeline with yourself

being in the present, the future being in front of you, and

the past being behind you, then you can easily alter each

part of the timeline by changing the scenario;

"I would buy juice if I had the money." I would have

bought juice if I had gotten paid." "I will have bought

juice by the time the store closes." "I had already bought

juice when he arrived."

Such scenarios are easy to picture and describe in your

native language, and eventually will be in your new

language. I recommend learning the verb conjugations

in a few tenses such as present, future, and past, yet

simply talking about yourself just like I did above. After

you have mastered the "I" form, move on to the next one.

Most verb charts show the conjugations listed by

pronouns, such as I buy, you buy, he/she buys, they buy,

we buy, you all buy. Memorizing them in that way can be monotonous. The best way to understand each conjugation is to be able to picture the scenario and understand how to describe the action.

When I was learning my first foreign language, I was excited to learn each new verb because I could immediately learn how to say it in the present, future, and past tense, meaning I could learn three new words instead of one simply by conjugating. When I first started to study verbs, I was presented with all the different names of the tenses, which bored me to no end. Instead of focusing on what the verb tense was called, I would skip straight to the verb and pay attention to the conjugation. I would picture a scenario in which I could use said conjugation and move on with my learning. I'm fluent in several languages and to this day I still don't know the names of all the tenses. That may shock you, but if you think about it, it doesn't really matter. Do you think about the names of the verb tenses you are using when you speak your native language? Probably not.

When I studied English in grade school, learning grammar rules, verb conjugations, and parts of speech really bored me. Understanding meaning and observing proper usage is what helped me understand the rules. I learned what made sense, and poor grammar stood out to me. If something was spoken or written with poor grammar, it just didn't feel or sound right. Even today it be real obvious when someone speak with bad grammar.

As you may remember, I learned Portuguese and Spanish without a course. I became fluent mostly by speaking with natives. I learned most of the grammar rules by paying attention to the conversation, and later thinking about concepts that I had learned. Whenever I learned how to say something, I simply paid attention to the way it was said. If it was a verb, I noticed how it ended. If it was a pronoun, I paid attention to the placement. If the noun required an article, I noticed it was there. Simple. By doing this, I was able to absorb many of the grammar rules and apply them to new thoughts and ideas in the language. If it was something that I didn't quite understand, I would ask questions until I fully understood it. I would often spend time pondering different phrases and mentally analyze the grammar involved. I would come up with different language scenarios in my mind and imagine myself talking to a native speaker. I would practice speaking with my imaginary friend until I could figure out why certain things are said in certain ways.

With all that being said, there is a difference between fluency and sophistication. When I decided to become an interpreter, I learned very quickly that I lacked sophistication in my language skills. The best way for me to remedy that was by improving my grammar and increasing my vocabulary. In other words, I had to learn how to speak and write at a level that an adult native would. Using grammar workbooks was helpful, but it was still an attempt to learn by analysis, which didn't fully help me to be able to produce the language at the level of a native speaker.

One thing I did to help me reach higher levels of fluency was purchase books on idioms and slang, as well as verb books. They did help some, but I still didn't feel like what I was learning was becoming a part of me, since I was merely learning examples of the language. I figured that the best way was to use authentic language sources; written and spoken language produced by natives. If I could learn to fully comprehend and reproduce the language in the same way as it was produced by natives, then I would eventually reach native-like fluency.

The turning point was when I decided to use monolingual sources for learning. I began to research grammar concepts by searching the terms only in the foreign language, reading about the grammar rules in the same language. By simply typing the foreign word for "grammar" into a search bar, I could easily access monolingual websites designed to help native speakers of the language improve their grammar. I recommend that you do the same thing.

I've mentioned the concept of shadowing several

times in this book. Shadowing has been by far the best thing to help me build my sophistication in a language. If I can successfully shadow a passage, maintaining the proper speed, intonation, and pronunciation as the speaker, while at the same time understanding everything that I'm repeating, then I am reproducing the language at the level of a native speaker.

Granted I am only referring to my performance of what is being shadowed. If I can shadow audio clips on certain subjects but cannot do so on other topics, then I'm in no way considering myself to have native-like fluency. Again, doing this would be easy to do in my native language. I would have little difficulty shadowing just about any news program, podcast, talk show, audiobook, sermon, lecture, or any other recorded speech in my native language. The only time I may have trouble would be if the topic was specialized and in a field that I have had no experience with, such as engineering.

When you make your first few attempts at shadowing in the foreign language, you may be shocked at just how difficult it is to reproduce the language at this level. The best way to overcome this difficulty is by taking very small segments and working on those until you've mastered them. I'm talking about 10 to 30 seconds at a time. For example, if the passage you are shadowing is an audio commercial, it may last 1 minute, but be spoken so quickly that you can't possibly keep up your pace at first. Use the skip back feature on your playing device, and only focus on the first few words. If your device can skip backwards 10 seconds, then the whole audio clip should be mastered in 10 second cumulative blocks. The key is to set very small goals, such as being able to shadow for 10-30 seconds, then a minute, gradually moving up to several minutes.

It can be easy to become overwhelmed when building your shadowing skills. It might be a good idea to have a few different shadowing projects. Work a few minutes on one podcast, a few on an audiobook, and a few more on a tv show. The good news is, the more you shadow a certain passage, the more likely you are to memorize it, thereby causing the words to become a permanent part of your vocabulary.

An advanced technique that you can use to reach lingual sophistication is transcribing. Transcribe the same audios or videos that you are shadowing. This is incredibly difficult, but it increases your listening skills. If a written version of that which you are transcribing is available, only use it as a last resort. Once you have transcribed a portion of the track, go back and shadow what you've transcribed. After you have made some progress with your transcribing skills, you'll be amazed at how much you have increased your skills in the language.

The point of these exercises is to get you to the level at which you can watch almost any show, movie, program or read any book or article without the need to look up any words, just as you are able to do in your native language. Once you have reached this level, you can proudly say that you have achieved native-like fluency in a now-not-so foreign language.

11 Polyglot

Juggling Multiple Languages

People always question how I manage to juggle so many languages. The truth is, it was something I had to learn how to do. In the beginning, I would go all-in while learning a new language, and neglect any previously learned language only to find that later on, when I was exposed to or forced to use a previously learned language, I had lost some basic skills and/or vocabulary. I guess the old saying, "If you don't use it, you lose it," is true after all.

Once I realized that this was the case, I tried desperately to come up with a way to keep learning new languages while not forgetting those that I had already learned. I tried many different studying schedules. I tried studying only one language per month for a while, but I found that a month was too much time between languages, and I would forget so much during the gaps. I then tried a language of the week schedule, which did work better, but I would end up longing for the other languages that weren't on the schedule, causing the current language of the week to lose its attractiveness. Then I tried doing two languages per day on a schedule but ended up running into the same types of issues. After some time, I found something that really works for me.

Nowadays, what I do is rather effective. I always have a priority language. It can be a language that I'm trying to become fluent in, or a language in which I'm trying to become certified. Either way, that language takes the stage every day. Most of my study time is taken up by that language. For the other languages that I've learned already, I simply spend a few minutes on each one every day. This process is quite therapeutic for me, as each language represents a different part of me. Each language seems to stimulate a different part of my psyche.

What I do with each language depends on the level of fluency I have in each one. Obviously, I strive to maintain contact with native speakers as much as possible. For languages that I have highly mastered, I simply expose myself to audios, videos, books, news, or anything that is authentic and used by natives. If it's audio, I usually shadow it. For those languages that I have majorly neglected in the past, I usually spend time reviewing course materials to dust off the old cobwebs. I also spend some time exposing myself to the language in its authentic form via podcasts or any of the sources that I've mentioned repeatedly thus far.

My problem has always been that I am absolutely in love with languages. All of them. In the beginning of my language journey, this caused me to start a language, pursue learning it to a degree, only then to become distracted by a new romance and run away with a new language affair. I wish that the wisdom that comes with age had been available to me back in my younger years, but I have yet to build a time machine with which I can remedy the mistakes of my past. In the past several years, I have come to the conclusion that since I am a language professional, working as an interpreter, my focus should be on that which will provide the next level of income for my family. It's only fair to them that I live this way, neglecting my fleeting desires to pursue that which will benefit us more in the long run. This decision is what caused me to spend so many years on Spanish to reach the level of certification that I have only recently achieved. I still dabble with those languages that I have only started learning, but only as a hobby. Luckily, my profession allows me to shoot for a higher level of mastery in each language, which is a new type of passion for me. Fluency used to be my goal in each language, but now it is mastery. I wish to achieve native-like fluency in as many languages as possible until my time runs out.

When I was learning my third language, a friend of mine told me a story of some missionaries that had visited his village back in Guatemala. A few of them claimed to have learned over 40 languages! My friend asked one of them how this was possible. The missionary replied that after you learn your second language, the third one is easier to learn. After that, each language you learn is easier than the previous. I've generally found this to be the case. After learning a few languages, I had figured out what the best approach for me was and knew in advance what obstacles would arise. The only exception to this is when it involves a language with sounds that are extremely different from those of my native language, especially if the written form does not use the Roman alphabet. Nevertheless, the challenge is less intimidating when approaching each new language.

If you are staring out on your multilingual journey, the

best advice I can give you is to refrain from neglecting that which you have learned. It doesn't have to be complicated. Simple daily exposure as well as frequent contact with natives will keep you current on your known languages. It's probably been a while since you had to study your native language, but you've probably been exposed to and have had to utilize it every day. It's the same thing with your second or third language.

Another great tip is to not assume that any new language will be similar to those you already know. If you know Italian, do not assume that Spanish will be easy. If you speak Portuguese, don't think that French will be similar. Many people make the mistake of trying to use what they know about one language to help them learn another. This usually causes a person to speak the new language incorrectly, because they have simply tried to morph the previously learned language into the new one. Approach each new language as something that is unknown to you and you will have better success.

I've heard and read over the years that learning multiple languages will make a person more intelligent, and will even increase a person's I.Q. While I'm not sure if either of those are true, I can say that I have noticed a difference in my mind over the years. The more I study and learn new languages, the sharper my mind seems to be. Also, there seems to be a higher sense of clarity in my ability to decipher puzzles or complex life situations. I've taken some free online I.Q. tests every couple of years since I first began learning different languages, and my score has increased every time. Although I'm not sure about the validity of such tests, I can say that there is an apparent change in my mind, and it continues to change. If it's an increase in intelligence or awareness, I'm not sure, but I do feel like I can think better than I could 10 years ago.

If you desire to become a polyglot, I would advise that you learn each language the correct way, as described in this book. Don't try to learn more than one new language at a time, as you will only make mediocre progress in any of them. If your ambition to become a polyglot causes even one language to suffer, then your own purpose has defeated you. Once you fall in love with language-learning, this will be your greatest temptation. Simply give each language the time that it deserves. It's better to speak a few like a native than it is to sound like a beginner in several.

Do not neglect your pronunciation for a moment. I love watching videos of polyglots that speak each language beautifully, striving to speak and sound like a native. On the other hand, I can't stand to listen to people that post videos of themselves butchering several languages. I'm sure their intentions are pure, but it's just not attractive to me to hear a person speak a language with a horrible accent.

Perhaps my standards are higher than those of many people, but to me language is an art, and should be pursued with deep passion. I'm not sure how many languages I will be able to learn throughout my lifetime. However, I do know that in each one that I claim to have achieved fluency, I will strive to make sure that the words pour out of my mouth just as if I were a native speaker since my goal is to stay true to the sounds of each language. I wouldn't necessarily expect you to develop such an overwhelming obsession for languages as I have, but I do ask that you treat each new language with the same openness and interest as you did in your first. The sky's the limit when it comes to how many languages you can learn. One day, I hope to personally welcome you to the small world of polyglots, and hopefully that world doesn't remain small for much longer.

12 Mouth of Babes

Teaching Children Languages

After a fellow interpreter and good friend of mine, Earl Rogers, introduced me to the world of interpreting, he told me about an interpreter he met that was fluent in seven languages. She had told Earl that her parents spoke with her and her siblings in a different language every week when she was growing up. Everyone in the household was required to speak the language of the week. This was before I got married and had kids, but I remember thinking that those parents had done something very special for their kids. Each one grew up with an ability that they could use to earn income, and have no problem finding employment. They also had a unique perspective on life and other people, as language and culture are so deeply intertwined.

A year before I became certified by the courts, my wife and I found out that we were going to have a baby. I was so excited to become a father, especially when we later discovered that our first baby was a little girl. I wondered what it would be like to love, provide for, and raise a child into adulthood. I also wondered if I had what it takes to provide for her. My wife, Alicia, and I had no life insurance, or savings. We had no way to make sure that she would be ok if something were to happen to us. Financially, we had nothing to pass down to her.

I was working two jobs at the time; as an aspiring full-time interpreter, and a part-time guitar instructor. Both jobs were benefits of skills that I had acquired after having been exposed to and developed a passion for language and music. My mom taught music at the first school I attended and was the piano player at our church. She also gave piano lessons in people's homes throughout the week, most of the time taking my brother and me along. I started playing trumpet when my mom signed me up for band in sixth grade. I guess she wanted to pass down her passion and skill to me. I'm glad she did, because I immediately fell in love with playing music.

My dad was also a musician. He gave me his guitar when I was 12 and I became addicted right away. I've been a musician for over 20 years and have been able to experience a deep connection with music. For over 8 years I was able to use my music skills to provide income for my family. My parents gave me that opportunity, and I will forever be grateful. When I learned that I was going to become a father, I decided to teach my daughter music and language, the only two skills I really had.

I had already started writing this book when Alicia got pregnant and had been pondering how people learn their first language. I thought it would be really fascinating and exciting to watch my daughter learn to speak. I remembered about the polyglot interpreter and how her parents were mostly responsible for her having learned so many languages, so I started going to the library to research bilingualism and multilingualism in children.

I learned that early exposure is important, as a child's developing brain can record language sounds during the first ten months and remember them perfectly for the rest

of their life. I also learned that some bilingual children

tend to become more self-conscious once they start

school. That coupled with speaking and learning in

English all day at school sometimes would make the

child become a passive bilingual, which is basically

having a native like comprehension of a foreign

language, but limited speaking skills.

When Alicia's gynecologist told us that our baby

could hear, I made an MP3 playlist of audio books and

music in as many foreign languages I could find, along

with some classical music. Alicia would put headphones

on her belly throughout the day, and our daughter, Alia,

would usually respond to the sounds. When she was

born, I burned the files to CDs, and we played the them

in her room at night while she slept.

My first words to Alia were in Spanish. I had decided to speak to her in a different language every three days and expose her to as many languages as possible before she reached the age of 10 months. When she was 3 months old, she started becoming interested in watching television. Alicia and I ran with this opportunity. I purchased several language learning DVDs for children, including some that claimed to teach babies how to read English. While I was at work, Alicia would put them on for Alia to watch throughout the day. Alicia was very supportive of my plan and would follow my language schedule when I wasn't home. When I got home from work, I would spend as much time as possible playing games, listening to music, reading books, and watching her DVDs with her. The more I participated in the activities, the more engaged she became.

I also purchased many different bedtime story books in foreign languages and would read to her every night at bedtime. My wife would also spend a lot of time reading to Alia in English. At every possible opportunity, I would expose Alia to native speakers of different languages. When we played together, I would count in different languages, according to the schedule, and incorporate the numbers with each activity. Whenever I would rock her to sleep, I would count in whichever language we were working on.

Many of our friends ridiculed us for attempting to teach Alia multiple languages. They claimed that we would only confuse her, and that she would have a hard time learning English. On the contrary, Alia thrived early on in her language skills. She started speaking at around 6 months. By the time she was 9 months old, she had already begun to read in English. Her first 10 words or so were in several different languages. By the time she was a year old, she could count to 10 in English, French, Arabic, Spanish, German, Mandarin, Italian, and Portuguese. By the time she was 2 years old she could read and speak basic symbols in Chinese. At 2 1/2, she memorized every single book and language DVD in her possession. During that time, she started sitting on my lap whenever I was studying foreign languages on my laptop and would usually take over the mousepad so that she could do the lessons instead.

When Alia turned 3, she told us that she was bored and wanted to go to school. We tried to explain to her that she was too young, but she refused to understand the concept of age limitation. We ended up hiring our friend, Neil Edwards, a teacher who owns a local private

178

school, to tutor her after hours. He would sit and read with her, as well as teach her basic mathematical concepts. After a few tutoring sessions, Neil told us that Alia was reading first grade level books. Neil did a great job working with Alia. Unfortunately, she became bored with her tutoring sessions after a few months and decided she didn't want to continue.

When Alia was 4, our bedtime stories, at her request, consisted of us reading from college level textbooks in Spanish, Portuguese, and Italian. Her intellect was at such a high level that new people we met would shockingly tell us that speaking with Alia was almost like speaking to an adult. At the same age, she once borrowed my wife's tablet and sent messages to almost all of our contacts. Those who replied ended up being engaged in messaging sessions that lasted several hours.

She would borrow Alicia's phone and text me in English and in other languages while I was at work. She memorized every cartoon and movie that she would watch. She would speak to us on a level that often scared us, asking us deep philosophical questions about life, death, God, sickness, wealth, poverty, and anything else that popped into her still-developing mind.

When Alia started school, her teachers and principals were amazed at her mental abilities. During kindergarten she was placed in an advanced reading class. In first grade, her test scores showed that she was reading at an eighth-grade level. Our night-time reading routines morphed into more advanced activities, primarily interpreting and sight-translating foreign language texts, as well as practicing dialogues from foreign language workbooks.

The thing I feared, her becoming a passive multilingual, started happening sometime during kindergarten. She began to become very self-conscious and refused to speak in any foreign language in front of anyone besides me. At the time I'm writing this she is 8 years old, and foreign languages are reserved for private conversations between her and me only, primarily occurring at home. I hope that as she continues to mature, she will gain self-confidence and indifference to the opinions of others, and flourish in her language abilities. I knew from the beginning that one day she would make the choice as to whether or not she wanted to pursue language learning. I realize that it's her choice, and I don't plan on being the polyglot dictator like the parents whom I described at the beginning of this chapter, as I feel it may rob my children of creativity.

Yes, I said children.

After I became a certified court interpreter, my income increased drastically. I had never made a high level of income before and did not know how to handle money. I purchased an SUV for Alicia that cost us more per month than our mortgage payment. Soon thereafter, we built another house to better suit our desires. Right after we closed on the new house loan, we found out that we had a wonderful little surprise on the way.

When Miah was born, I was still working two jobs. Since we had accumulated more expenses, my interpreting income still had to be supplemented somehow. When our expenses increased again with the cost of providing for a new child, I rented a small studio nearby our house and started giving language lessons. I also began to give guitar lessons out of our home and language lessons via Skype. In short, I filled my time with work. A few months after Miah was born, Alicia and I joined a network marketing business in hopes that our financial problems would go away. This resulted in me being home even less often.

With the craziness of my new schedule, not being home much, I missed out on those valuable first few years with Miah. I tried to repeat the process that we followed with Alia, but it was impossible. On top of that, Miah was a different type of child. She had more energy than anyone I had ever met, and still does. She was more interested in physical activities than reading. In fact, she just recently sat still enough to let me read a book to her for the first time, at 6 years old.

Miah kicked, twisted, turned, and danced inside the womb during almost the whole pregnancy. When she was born, it was as if she wasn't going to let her underdeveloped body stop her from being active. She started lifting her head off the floor almost right away, was able to sit herself up at 2 months, and as soon as she figured out how to pull herself up to standing position in her crib, she learned to escape. We couldn't keep any electronics in her room, such as the CD player that I was hoping to use to help her language skills, because she took everything apart. She was so interested in doing things with her hands. We would often walk into the living room to find video game system remotes stacked vertically on top one another, a feat that I still have difficulty with. She was so active that she refused to watch any of the language DVDs that we put on for her. It seemed like I was not going to be able to teach her languages after all. Probably the only advantage we did have was being able to expose Miah to native speakers of Spanish during our business building years, since most of our business partners and colleagues were Hispanic.

When she was about 4 years old, Alicia and I finally overcame our financial situation after I decided to interpret full time. I was finally able to be home every evening and decided to reattempt teaching Miah. She didn't like to sit in front of a computer and would not sit still long enough for me to teach her using flash cards or books. One day, I finally figured out a way to teach her languages. All she ever wants to do is play, so I decided to make language learning fun for her. Miah is very strong willed, so I had to be quite creative. I decided to teach her only Spanish for a while, since she was so resistant at first.

When she realized we could have fun and learn

Spanish at the same time, she began to learn rather quickly. I did teach her to count as well as to say some basic phrases in a few other languages, such as *good morning, good night,* and *I love you,* but she really likes "playing" with me in Spanish, so that's what I'm developing in her until I feel like she's ready to take on another language. I have no doubt that I will be able to teach her several other languages, provided I keep it fun and teach her based on how she wants to learn.

The reason I wrote this chapter is because so many people have asked me how to teach their children foreign languages. Many more have expressed to me that the reason they are learning a new language is so they can teach their children. There are several obvious benefits that a child will have if they grow up knowing more than one language. If you are one of those parents who wishes for their child to grow up bilingual or multilingual, then the following is the best advice I can give.

Make sure you expose your children to native speakers often. Also expose them to audios and videos of the language. If you are a native speaker of the language you want your child to learn, speak to them in that language. They'll learn it. If you're not a native, but have attained almost perfect pronunciation, then the same applies. If you are using videos, engage with your child. Participate. Make it fun. Always remember, just like I had to, that all kids are different.

13 Grand Finale

If you have made it this far, I personally thank you for taking the time to read this book. Most of the concepts taught in this book I learned from observing my children learn how to speak, many conversations and interviews I had with language learners of all ages, countless language lessons I've given over the years, as well as the simple observation that regardless of having studied one or more foreign languages, most people are still unilingual. My hope is that you will take the concepts in this book and apply them to learning one or more new languages. If you, like most people, have already had a bad or unsuccessful experience with any language, it's ok to start over from scratch. At least by doing it in an effective way this time, you will be able to get the results you desire.

To recap what has been covered, you must approach learning a new language in a similar fashion to the way you learned your first. You were exposed to the language in its authentic form, being produced by natives. You listened constantly, permeating your awareness with the sounds of the language. You used your perfectly capable human speech organs to gradually learn to reproduce the sounds you heard while being coached by natives. Eventually you were able to sound like a native speaker. After building your fluency to a degree, you learned how to read and write the sounds that you had been speaking. You also learned the basics of grammar and continued upon a path of literal development until you eventually reached a point of mastery, in other words, a native-like fluency.

I believe that this is possible for anyone to achieve in a second, third, or even tenth language. I've not only experienced it myself, but I've witnessed other people achieve the same. If you find yourself struggling with believing that you too are able to become bilingual or multilingual, then I encourage you to dig deep within yourself. The truth is you can learn any language you want. It may take lots of work, but that's ok. The accomplishment will be well worth it.

I'm not sure what caused you to pursue learning a foreign language. Maybe you want to travel. Maybe you want a promotion. For me, it was simply something I stumbled upon, and quickly developed into a passion. Learning languages has opened my eyes to see through cultural walls, which many times cause so much conflict. I was raised in a society in which foreign immigrants are looked down upon and criticized. I unknowingly grew up with a bit of racism within me. That began to change once I started learning foreign languages from natives.

One night on the job at the turkey plant, I was having a conversation with a Hispanic migrant worker. He explained to me that he had left his wife and kids in his home country more than five years prior and hadn't seen any of them since. He worked 6–7 days a week, 8–10 hours per day making minimum wage. He lived in a single-wide trailer with three or four other migrant workers and sent almost all of his money back home to support his family. In the U.S. he lived as meager a lifestyle as possible so that his family, which he wasn't even around, could survive.

I came home from work that night in tears. I couldn't believe how wrong my mindset had been about Hispanics and their culture. They are a self-sacrificing, family-oriented, humble, and hard-working people. Had I not learned Spanish, I might never have learned that. Similar things have happened with other languages. I was taught growing up that most Arabs are full of hatred towards Americans, and most wanted to even kill us all. Once I began learning Arabic and making friends with Arabs, I found that not to be the case. They are people just like you and me. They have families, feelings, dreams, ambitions, and fears. Sure, their religion may differ from mine or yours, but that doesn't make the stereotypes you hear about them true.

I could list many more examples of experiences that I've had with native speakers from different parts of the world. With each foreign person I befriended, more preconceived prejudices about their cultures were dispelled. On my first trip to Switzerland, one of my friends watched me interact with people from at least nine different countries. He mentioned to me that it was amazing how they opened up to me once I started speaking their language with them. He even recommended that I write a book called *How to Befriend a Nation*. That conversation has stuck with me over the years.

I could go on and on about racism and overall hatred of other cultures. The thing I've come to learn is we are all people, and language is one thing that unites people. I believe that if more people were to learn foreign languages, ultimately embracing the culture of the people who speak them, more and more cultural boundaries would come down. There would be less conflict between cultures that simply don't understand one another. I'm not saying that I believe this philosophy could ultimately heal the world and end all wars, but it certainly could help.

Regardless of your reasons for learning one or more new languages, I encourage you to keep going no matter how tough it may seem at times. Don't let yourself become discouraged. Don't accept that it is impossible, or even improbable, for you to reach your goal of achieving native-like fluency. Always remind yourself that the fact that you can read this means you are a language master. You've done it before. You can do it again.

Thank you for reading!! Please don't forget to

leave a review online and subscribe to my

mailing list at

www.howtoreallylearnalanguage.com

CPSIA information can be obtained
at www.ICGtesting.com
Printed in the USA
LVHW041218011020
667641LV00003B/177

9 781087 866086